WOMEN'S RESILIENCE IN THE LAO PEOPLE'S DEMOCRATIC REPUBLIC

HOW LAWS AND POLICIES PROMOTE GENDER EQUALITY IN CLIMATE CHANGE AND DISASTER RISK MANAGEMENT

JUNE 2022

ASIAN DEVELOPMENT BANK

ADB

Contents

Tables, Figure, and Boxes

Foreword

The impact of climate change and disasters is contingent on various socioeconomic factors as well as country laws, policies, and decisions by policymakers. Gender roles and social inequalities in access to resources, care responsibilities, and lower levels of education systematically disadvantage women and girls, rendering them more vulnerable to the impact of climate change and disasters. Numerous reports have revealed disproportionately higher mortality rates among women and girls during disasters, further highlighting that this area of work requires closer attention from governments and development partners.*

The Asian Development Bank (ADB) works with developing member country stakeholders with a shared vision to strengthen approaches to address climate change and improve disaster resilience through investments in water supply, sanitation, irrigation, flood control, transport, and energy, as well as to increase knowledge sharing and cooperation with partners in the region. It is understood that a "business as usual" approach no longer works for tackling increasingly complex problems in Asia and the Pacific. A holistic and truly cross-sector and thematic approach is needed, with gender equality being a central consideration for the effectiveness and sustainability of climate change and disaster risk management (CCDRM) actions.

ADB has been promoting "integrated approaches" and working to mainstream gender equality and women's empowerment in operations to support developing member countries in their efforts to become resilient to climate change and disaster. Improved gender equality and women's empowerment turn into positive benefits for many other development goals and targets. The ADB Strategy 2030 Operational Plan for Priority Two on Accelerating Gender Equality outlines a clear vision of gender equality as an effective means for achieving sustainable and inclusive growth, including in the area of climate and disaster resiliency.

This Lao People's Democratic Republic (Lao PDR) country report is part of a series of publications that applies the National Good Practice Framework presented in the regional report *Gender-Inclusive Legislative Framework and Laws to Strengthen Women's Resilience to Climate Change and Disasters,* to explore the extent of integration of gender considerations in CCDRM laws, policies and plans in Fiji, the Lao PDR, and Mongolia. It was prepared under a regional knowledge and support technical assistance project on Strengthening Women's Resilience to Climate Change and Disaster Risk in Asia and the Pacific. The project specifically aims to increase the capacity of these three countries to develop and advance gender-responsive CCDRM national and sector policies and laws. It also contributes to the wider thrust of the ADB Gender Equality Thematic Group to promote national legislation that supports women's resilience through gender-inclusive approaches to CCDRM.

---

* S. Brown et al. 2019. Gender and Age Inequality of Disaster Risk: *Research Paper*. UNICEF and UN Women.

This report is important as ADB commitments are turned into actions. In light of the increasing complexity of climate and disaster risk challenges in the Asia and Pacific region, it adds to the understanding of gaps, as well as good practices in CCDRM laws and policies, and provides recommendations for moving forward. This report should serve as valuable input to support government agencies and policymakers in the Lao PDR to make country laws and policies gender-responsive and supportive to women's resilience to climate change and disasters.

Samantha Hung
Chief of Gender Equality Thematic Group
Sustainable Development and Climate Change Department
Asian Development Bank

Acknowledgments

This report is based on work undertaken under under the Asian Development Bank (ADB) Technical Assistance (TA) 9348-REG: *Strengthening Women's Resilience to Climate Change and Disaster Risk in Asia and the Pacific*. Overall, the regional project objective is to strengthen the capacity of policymakers in three countries: Fiji, the Lao People's Democratic Republic (Lao PDR), and Mongolia, and to make climate change and disaster risk management (DRM) policies, strategies, or financing more gender-responsive. This Lao PDR country report on climate change and DRM law and policy frameworks is one element of the project, and similar reports have been prepared for Fiji and Mongolia.

The report was prepared under the overall guidance of Malika Shagazatova (social development specialist) and Zonibel Woods (senior social development specialist) of the ADB Sustainable Development and Climate Change Department (SDCC). Support and contributions were provided by Alih Faisal Pimentel Abdul (TA coordinator), Phothong Siliphong (national gender consultant), Ma. Celia A. Guzon (senior operations assistant), and Theonakhet Saphakdy (senior social development officer) of the ADB Lao PDR Resident Mission. Consultants Robyn Layton (gender and law expert) and Mary Picard (climate change and disaster risk management/environmental law expert) drafted the report. The report was edited by Amy Reggers, gender and climate change consultant.

Special thanks to Samantha Hung, chief of gender equality thematic group, SDCC; and Sonomi Tanaka, country director, the Lao People's Democratic Republic and former chief of gender equity thematic group, SDCC, for their overall support and guidance in the implementation of the TA.

The report benefited significantly from comments by Ninpaseuth Xayaphonesy, director general of the Department of Women in Development, Lao Women's Union; and Inthana Bouphasavanh, director of the Association for Development of Women and Legal Education in the Lao PDR.

Special thanks for the contributions of participants in two national workshops in the Lao PDR.

Abbreviations

ADB	Asian Development Bank
CBDRR	community-based disaster risk reduction
CC Decree	Decree on Climate Change 2019
CEDAW Committee	Committee on the Elimination of Discrimination Against Women
CEDAW Convention	Convention on the Elimination of All Forms of Discrimination Against Women
CEDAW GR37	CEDAW General Recommendation No. 37 on Gender-related dimensions of disaster risk reduction in the context of climate change
DCC	Department of Climate Change
DM Law	Law on Disaster Management 2019
DRR	Disaster Risk Reduction
EIA	environmental impact assessment
EIA Decree	Decree on Environmental Impact Assessment 2019
FAO	Food and Agriculture Organization of the United Nations
GBV	gender-based violence
GCF	Green Climate Fund
ILO	International Labour Organization
IPU	Inter-Parliamentary Union
Lao PDR	Lao People's Democratic Republic
LGE	Law on Gender Equality 2019
LWU	Lao Women's Union
MAF	Ministry of Agriculture and Forestry

MLSW	Ministry of Labor and Social Welfare
MoNRE	Ministry of Natural Resources and Environment
MSMEs	micro, small, and medium-sized enterprises
NAPA	National Adaptation Program of Action on Climate Change
NAPGE	National Action Plan on Gender Equality (2021–2025)
NDC	Nationally Determined Contribution
NEC	National Environment Committee
NSDRR	National Disaster Risk Reduction Strategy 2021–2030 (under development)
NSEDP	National Socioeconomic Development Plan
NTFP	Non-Timber Forest Products
SDG	Sustainable Development Goal (17 goals in the UN 2030 Agenda)
UN	United Nations
UNDP	United Nations Development Programme
UNDRR	United Nations Office for Disaster Risk Reduction
UNFCCC	United Nations Framework Convention on Climate Change
UNFPA	United Nations Population Fund
UNICEF	United Nations Children's Fund
UXO	unexploded ordnance
VAW	violence against women
WFP	World Food Programme

Executive Summary

The Lao People's Democratic Republic (Lao PDR) faces significant sustainability and environmental challenges that are amplified by climate change. While the Lao PDR is not as highly exposed to natural hazards as its neighbors, its limited economic resources create challenges for disaster management and climate change adaptation. Hydrological hazards such as flooding, droughts, and storms frequently impact rural areas, affecting the agricultural livelihoods on which most of the population relies. They also cause disease outbreaks, threaten food security, and force communities to migrate due to concerns for personal safety and the security of their livelihoods. Most of the land in the Lao PDR is degraded due to the impacts of droughts, flooding, and landslides, as well as the unsustainable use of natural resources, which has been accelerated by the marketization of agriculture. As a country with approximately 60% forest cover, the Lao PDR aims to strike a balance between the economic benefits of the forestry industry and the climate change mitigation and adaptation benefits of forest conservation.

Nearly three-quarters of households in the Lao PDR are engaged in agriculture, a sector highly vulnerable to the impacts of climate change and disasters. In devastating floods in 2018, the agriculture sector—including fisheries and forestry—suffered nearly 60% of the total economic losses.[a] Climate projections for the Lao PDR indicate more frequent and destructive droughts, storms, and floods in the future due to longer hot and dry periods and an increase in mean average rainfall that will likely cause more intense periods of rainfall in the wet season. Due to a complex topography, the Lao PDR has over 40 unique livelihood groups, each with different vulnerabilities to the impacts of natural hazards and climate change. The most vulnerable groups are those dependent on highland rice paddies, as the rugged terrain in these areas limits access to productive land and opportunities to diversify livelihoods. Climate change will bring challenges for the Lao PDR including rural impoverishment, food insecurity, migration, and changes in work and education opportunities that also impact family relations and work-related gender roles. These challenges can negatively impact the overall gender equality situation.

The Lao PDR has increased the education rates of girls and has made progress in the representation of women in managerial and senior roles in both the public and private sectors. However, high rates of violence against women and children persist, and as reporting is uncommon, victims/survivors often do not have access to justice. Compared to men, women also have poor employment opportunities and working conditions, as well as limited access to land and financial capital. These key areas of socioeconomic development are likely to be exacerbated further with the rise in climate and disaster-related risks. Therefore, alongside the challenges of combating disaster and climate impacts, it is crucial to ensure that women's socioeconomic resilience is increased so that women and men move forward with increased equality of outcomes. This requires a focus, not only on how climate and disaster-related laws and policies can be more gender responsive but also on improving gender equality in key socioeconomic areas that impact women's resilience.

The purpose of this report was to conduct a gender analysis of the national legal and policy frameworks of the Lao PDR to determine whether laws, policies, and strategies consider gender inequalities as they relate to climate and disaster risk and contribute to strengthening women's resilience. The laws of a country set the legal framework and provide the foundation to regulate a sector and guarantee fundamental rights and policies should further

---

[a] Government of Lao PDR. 2018. *Post-Disaster Needs Assessment (PDNA) 2018 Floods Lao PDR*. Vientiane.

amplify legal provisions and implement legislative guarantees. A National Good Practice Legislative Framework was developed for the analysis in this report. The framework draws on (i) the Committee on the *Elimination of Discrimination Against Women (CEDAW) General Recommendation No. 37* on the gender-related dimensions of disaster risk reduction in the context of climate change (CEDAW GR37), and (ii) a report on best practice legal frameworks in Asia and the Pacific, which assists in selecting laws and policies related to the national approach to gender equality, climate and disaster risks, as well as socioeconomic development to be gender analyzed. The analysis of the selected laws and policies informed an assessment of the extent to which equality and discrimination concepts are explicit in laws and policies and how this affects women's resilience to climate and disaster risks. The report methodology included secondary data collection and analysis, support by a country mission, stakeholder interviews, and national workshops.

Results of the analysis found that the Law on Gender Equality 2019 (LGE) is gender responsive, with some gender positive provisions, as it incorporates important equality principles and provides for overcoming cultural beliefs that inhibit women's advancement. Crucially, it mandates gender mainstreaming in laws and policies across all areas of work. The law is accompanied by an ambitious policy for implementation—the National Action Plan on Gender Equality 2021–2025 (NAPGE)—which is gender responsive and includes a broad spectrum of gender positive targets, such as introducing quotas for women and girls over a broad spectrum of activities including leadership roles in the areas such as climate change and disaster risk reduction. With more detailed action plans for each set of targets and new complaints procedures, the law and action plan can support effective integration of gender considerations and an increase in the participation of women in decision making on issues relating to resilience to climate change and disasters.

Despite these achievements, the analysis reveals that there is a notable lack of commitments to equality and nondiscrimination in key laws and policies related to disaster risk management, environment, and climate change. The laws and policies of the Lao PDR in these areas are based on formal equality between men and women, but do not address gender inequality and gender differences in risks or needs or provide mechanisms for the collection of sex-disaggregated data, gender analysis, gender mainstreaming, or the specific engagement of women in their institutions and processes. A notable exception is the Decree on Environmental Impact Assessments 2019 (EIA Decree), which mandates the collection of information and conduct of assessments relating to gender. Another positive step forward is the inclusion of the Lao Women's Union (LWU) in the Technical Working Group on Climate Change, which promotes the participation of women in environmental policy making. LWU is also included in Village Disaster Management Committees under the Law on Disaster Management (DM Law), although not in the district, provincial, or central DM Committee. The capacity of LWU to influence women's resilience through these mechanisms is also limited by the lack of any specific gender criteria or targets in the relevant law and policy frameworks. Similar findings from a close analysis of agriculture sector laws and policies reveal no integration of gender equality and nondiscrimination principles and no mention of the gender dimensions of agriculture considered in related laws or policies. The one exception is the *National Agro-Biodiversity Program and Action Plan 2021–2025*, which goes some way towards gender sensitivity by acknowledging the different roles of men and women in managing and using agro-biodiversity resources and calls for their knowledge to be incorporated into management plans.

In addition to sector-specific laws and policies, several laws governing socioeconomic areas which can contribute to building women's resilience to climate change and disaster risk were analyzed. The report focuses on three areas (i) combating gender-based violence (GBV), (ii) improving women's access to assets, and (iii) increasing women's access to decent work. Findings reveal that both the Law on Preventing and Combatting Violence against Women and Children 2014 and the Law on Development and Protection of Women 2004 promote the settlement and mediation of violence against women, which is contrary to international best practice as outlined in CEDAW General Recommendations Numbers 33 and 35. The National Plan of Action on Protection and Elimination of Violence Against Women and Children (2021–2025) represents a positive step forward in terms of collecting data on victims/survivors of GBV, which can be used to design gender-responsive measures. With women's access to assets, the report findings note that as of 2021 no laws or policies about land tenure and inheritance (women's access to assets) include concepts of equality and nondiscrimination. Given the influence of patrilineal traditional inheritance customs that preference sons over daughters—and the fact that most rural land users do not have legal documentation for land tenure—gender-responsive laws and policies in this area are crucial. Finally, with decent work for women, the analysis found several areas of concern that are not explicitly addressed by sector law or policy, or where the laws and policies perpetuate discrimination. These include workplace sexual harassment, the gender pay gap, and barriers to women's access to minimum wage and financial capital.

In conclusion, the report finds that sector laws and policies that affect women's resilience to climate change and disasters in the Lao PDR are not yet gender mainstreamed. The exception is the Decree on Environmental Impact Assessment 2019 (EIA Decree), which is classified as gender sensitive, as it supports the collection of gender-related information. However, its impact is likely to be limited without a comprehensive set of laws and policies to clearly define and enforce commitments to gender equality across a range of environmental and socioeconomic issue areas. The LGE and the NAPGE can serve as useful starting points in this regard. The report includes a set of specific and general recommendations to address some of the gaps in the Lao PDR law and policy framework.

Specific Recommendations:

(i) **Develop gender responsive guidance to accompany the Law on Gender Equality** to define key concepts and complement the National Action Plan on Gender Equality, laying the foundation for gender responsive implementation measures across all sectors.

(ii) **Support women's participation in decision making in the National Strategy on Climate Change (2021–2030) and future reviews of the Climate Change Decree** to generate gender responsive climate change measures and meet the NAPGE's ambitious targets for women's participation and leadership in climate change decision making.

(iii) **Integrate measures to support women's resilience in the implementation of the Law on Disaster Management through the National Strategy on Disaster Risk Reduction (DRR) and its 5-year action plans**, to address women's participation in DRR, and differential needs in disaster contexts, including support for women living in rural areas and other high-risk situations.

(iv) **Support women's resilience through the right to live without violence with revisions to the Law on Preventing and Combatting Violence against Women and Children 2014 and strong implementation of the National Plan of Action on Protection and Elimination of Violence Against Women and Children (2021–2025).**

(v) **Enhance women's economic capacity through changes to the wage equality provisions in the Law on Labor (2014),** by making a new law on the prevention of harassment and violence in the workplace and investing in the development of women-led micro, small, and medium-sized enterprises (MSMEs).

(vi) **Improve women's access to land, housing, and agricultural resources through gender mainstreaming the Law on Land 2019, the Law on Resettlement and Vocation 2018, the Law on Forestry 2007**, and the National Agro-Biodiversity Program and Action Plan (2021-2025).

General Recommendations:

(i) **Collection and analysis of disaggregated data needs to be prioritized.**

(ii) **Increasing women's participation in DRR, climate change adaptation, and environmental decision making is essential.**

(iii) **Consolidate a gender responsive approach to climate change and disaster risk policy development and implementation.**

1 Background

There is increasing global political consensus that the transition to cleaner, more sustainable development includes not only increasing the number of women in climate and environment related decision making but also promoting gender equality as part of climate action and disaster risk management. Gender equality and social inclusion are increasingly seen as essential to sustainable development and a just transition to a low-carbon climate future.

Key international treaties recommend or mandate the inclusion of gender equality indicators as part of the reporting obligations of State Parties and some treaty bodies are leading by example through gender action plans. Under the United Nations Framework Convention on Climate Change (UNFCCC), a gender action plan includes targets for increased representation and participation of women in UNFCCC processes, a gender balance goal at intergovernmental meetings, and guidance for State Parties in their efforts to integrate gender equality issues into their national commitments, reporting processes and plans. These efforts are translating into results; gender analysis of Nationally Determined Contributions (NDCs) in 2020 demonstrate that 50% of updated NDCs have a reference to gender or women, compared to only 33% in 2016, and several Parties that did not refer to gender in their 2016 submission now include references to gender, some in substantive ways. All of the new NDCs (countries that had not previously submitted any NDC) include a reference to women or gender.[1]

Similarly, within global disaster risk management efforts, the Sendai Framework for Disaster Risk Reduction (DRR), the Ha Noi Recommendations for Action on Gender and Disaster Risk Reduction, and the Ulaanbaatar Declaration of the 2018 Asian Ministerial Conference on Disaster Risk Reduction all recognize the importance of promoting the participation of women in decision making in DRR and ensuring gender-sensitive policies for disaster risk management. The Ulaanbaatar Declaration specifically called on all governments and stakeholders to:

> "Promote full and equal participation of women in leading, designing, and implementing gender-sensitive disaster risk reduction policies, plans and programmes, through joint efforts by public and private sector, supported by appropriate legal frameworks and allocation of necessary resources."[2]

Furthermore, the Committee for the Elimination of Discrimination Against Women (CEDAW Committee) is the treaty body of the long-standing Convention on the Elimination of All Forms of Discrimination Against Women (CEDAW Convention). It sets out in General Recommendation No. 37 the obligations of member States on the gender-related dimensions of disaster risk reduction in the context of climate change (CEDAW GR37). This outlines the requirement for national policies and plans to address gender inequalities, reduce disaster risk, and increase resilience to the adverse effects of climate change. The CEDAW Committee notes that the focus needs to go beyond climate change and disaster risk policies and plans to also include national socioeconomic development planning.

Despite growing recognition of the need to integrate gender equality and full and effective participation of women in climate change action and disaster risk management, a recent United Nations (UN) Women report notes that

---

[1]   Women's Environment and Development Organization. 2020. *Gender Climate Tracker: Quick Analysis.*
[2]   Asian Ministerial Conference on Disaster Risk Reduction. 2018. *Ulaanbaatar Declaration.* Ulaanbaatar.

inconsistencies remain in national legislation, policies, and plans.[3] Many countries still have gaps integrating their gender equality and women's empowerment commitments in climate change and disaster risk management legal frameworks, policies, and plans. These frameworks have a critical role in demonstrating national commitments, however the adequacy of such frameworks on gender equality is yet to be comprehensively reviewed. This report focuses on the Lao People's Democratic Republic (Lao PDR) and is part of a three-country series that includes Fiji and Mongolia. It contributes to addressing this gap by providing the results of a gender analysis of national law and policy frameworks to understand if and how they include gender equality concepts, and language to form a strong foundation for promoting women's resilience to climate change and disasters.

1.1   Introduction

The Lao PDR is facing the adverse effects of climate change and disasters. Economic losses from extreme weather and climate-related disasters have increased significantly in the Lao PDR since 2010.[4] The influence of climate change is projected to continue this trend by increasing the severity of the most frequent and destructive hazards: floods, storms, and droughts.[5] These disasters particularly impact rural areas in the Lao PDR, where much of the population engages in subsistence agriculture.[6] For example, the lowlands that produce the most rice in the Lao PDR are highly vulnerable to flooding, with significant consequences for rural livelihoods, food security, and health.[7]

Sudden disaster impacts are overwhelmingly negative, but the need to adapt to and mitigate climate change is a more mixed phenomenon that can also bring positive opportunities through the social changes it triggers. The limited economic resources of the Lao PDR create challenges for disaster management and climate change adaptation.[8] However, the country also has advantages; increased international demand for renewable energy has stimulated rapid growth in the Lao PDR hydropower sector, which accounts for nearly a third of the Lao PDR exports. Investment in hydropower has supported the rapid electrification of the country from 15% in 1995 to over 90% by 2016, improving opportunities and quality of life overall, although some remote rural areas had not been reached by 2019.[9] There are also future work opportunities in reforestation and forest conservation, which are a government priority for both climate change mitigation and adaptation.[10]

Important in the pursuit of climate adaptation and mitigation—as well as disaster risk management—is ensuring that both women and men are included, and that past gender inequality is addressed so that they can share equally in the benefits of risk-informed development. Gender inequalities in key socioeconomic areas in normal times can impact the ability of women to benefit from climate action and build resilience.[11] In the Lao PDR, structural gender inequality and discrimination against women exist in several socioeconomic spheres such as women's political representation and economic participation, as well as grave human rights violations such as gender-based violence (GBV). To address these issues and enable women to build resilience, gender equality and nondiscrimination

[3]   H. Nguyen et al. 2020. *Review of Gender Responsiveness and Disability Inclusion in Disaster Risk Reduction in Asia and the Pacific.* Bangkok: UN Women.
[4]   United Nations Office for Disaster Risk Reduction (UNDRR). 2019. *Disaster Risk Reduction in Lao PDR: Status Report 2019.* Bangkok.
[5]   World Bank Climate Change Knowledge Portal. 2020. *Lao People's Democratic Republic: Climate Data Projections* (accessed 7 February 2022).
[6]   Asian Development Bank (ADB). Key Indicator Data Base Lao PDR. https://data.adb.org/dataset/lao-pdr-key-indicators (accessed 2 June 2021); (accessed 2 June 2021); World Food Programme (WFP). 2017. Executive Board First Regular Session (20–23 February 2017). Rome, cited in WFP. 2017. Lao PDR Country Strategic Plan (2017–2021). Rome. para. 11.
[7]   Government of Lao PDR, Ministry of Natural Resources and Environment (MoNRE) and WFP. 2016. *Lao People's Democratic Republic, Consolidated Livelihood Exercise for Analyzing Resilience (CLEAR).* Vientiane.
[8]   Kindernothilfe, Medico international, Oxfam, Plan International, Terre des hommes and Welthungerhilfe. 2020. *World Risk Report 2020 - Focus: Forced Displacement and Migration.* Berlin.
[9]   ADB. 2019. *Lao People's Democratic Republic Energy Sector Assessment, Strategy, and Road Map.* Manila. p. 48.
[10] World Bank. 2021. *Lao PDR Signs Agreement to Protect Forests and Reduce Carbon Emissions.* 27 January.
[11] C. Pross et al. 2020. *Climate Change, Gender Equality and Human Rights in Asia: Regional Review and Promising Practices.* Bangkok. New York: UN Women.

principles need to be embedded in laws and policies and actively implemented in programs and activities, not only in those related to climate and disaster risks but also socioeconomic development.

In this report, key national laws and policies of the Lao PDR are analyzed to understand how they provide a legal foundation and explicit commitment to strengthening women's resilience. This is done by looking at the national commitments to promoting gender equality, analyzing climate and disaster risk management laws and policies—with a specific focus on agriculture—and analysis of selected socioeconomic areas that directly relate to building women's resilience including GBV prevention, rights to access to land and assets, and decent work.

1.2   Purpose and Scope

Gender differences in the impacts of climate change and disasters are related to both preexisting inequality and discrimination. Differentiated gender roles mean that hazards may impact women and men differently. In general, disasters exacerbate prior disadvantages, while climate change adaptation can provide new opportunities as well as potentially reinforce existing disadvantages. To minimize the adverse impacts of climate change and disasters and improve women's resilience to these risks, it is necessary to understand underlying gender inequality and discrimination against women.

The purpose of this report is to conduct a gender analysis of key elements of the national legal and policy framework of the Lao PDR to determine the extent to which laws, policies, and strategies consider gender equality and contribute to strengthening women's resilience to climate change and disaster risk. The report begins by presenting a framework for selecting and analyzing relevant laws and policies. The framework draws on CEDAW GR37 and builds on a national framework approach developed in a regional ADB report on best practices in legislation.[12] A country profile is presented to set the context—including key climate hazards and a description of the situation for women in the Lao PDR—with a focus on socioeconomic areas that impact resilience building. Then, a gender analysis is conducted of a range of laws and policies relevant to disaster risk management, climate change, the agriculture sector, and key areas of women's socioeconomic resilience. The report concludes with an analysis of the extent to which the laws and policies promote women's resilience and makes recommendations to enhance the inclusion of gender equality commitments in laws and policies to strengthen women's resilience to climate change and disasters.

The key aims of this report are to

(i)   outline a *National Good Practice Legislative Framework for Strengthening Women's Resilience to Climate Change and Disasters* which governments can use to analyze laws, policies, and institutions related to climate change and disaster risk management;

(ii)   apply the framework and present the analysis to the Government of the Lao People's Democratic Republic—in light of the national context and international standards—to determine how gender responsive laws and policies are; and

(iii)   make recommendations on how the government can enhance the commitment to gender equality through laws and policies that promote women's resilience through gender responsive climate change adaptation and disaster risk management.

---

[12]   ADB. 2021. *Gender-Inclusive Legislative Framework and Laws to Strengthen Women's Resilience to Climate Change and Disaster Risk.* Manila.

1.3   A National Good Practice Legislative Framework for Strengthening Women's Resilience to Climate Change and Disasters

To achieve the first aim of this report, a *National Good Practice Legislative Framework for Strengthening Women's Resilience to Climate Change and Disasters* was developed. The framework draws on the Convention on the Elimination of All Forms of Discrimination Against Women (CEDAW Convention) and CEDAW GR37. The CEDAW Convention is a binding international treaty that was adopted in 1979 by the UN General Assembly and is often described as an international bill of rights for women. Consisting of a preamble and 30 articles, it defines what constitutes discrimination against women and sets up an agenda for national action to end such discrimination.[13] The Lao PDR is a party to the CEDAW Convention without any current reservations.[14]

Given the global focus on climate change, disaster risk reduction, and the significant impact on human life and livelihood, the CEDAW Committee added CEDAW GR37 in 2018. CEDAW GR37 discusses how the different aspects of the CEDAW Convention apply to these risks and makes expert recommendations to State Parties on how to address each of them. It states, "the Committee has underlined that States parties and other stakeholders have obligations to take concrete steps to address discrimination against women in the fields of disaster risk reduction and climate change through the adoption of targeted laws, policies, mitigation and adaptation strategies, budgets and other measures."[15]

CEDAW GR37 underscores the general principles of the CEDAW Convention that are applicable: substantive equality and nondiscrimination, participation and empowerment, and accountability and access to justice. It notes special measures—such as disaggregated data collection by sex, age, disability, ethnicity, and geographical location and its use, policy coherence, capacity development, and alignment with extra-territorial obligations—that State Parties should prioritize in the pursuit of reducing disaster risk for women.[16] Overall, CEDAW GR37 outlines how an increase in women's resilience to climate change and disaster risks needs support from broader socioeconomic laws and policies as well as the realization of specific rights such as the right to live free from GBV, the right to work, social protection, and the right to health among others (footnote 18).

Building on the general principles of the CEDAW Convention, the specific areas of concern under CEDAW GR37—and the report on global good practice and international standards—Figure 1 presents the *National Good Practice Legislative Framework for Strengthening Women's Resilience to Climate Change and Disasters.*[17] When the framework is in place, the institutional mandates, policies, and strategies have a solid legal base. They can in turn support gender-responsive resource allocation decisions and the use of gender analysis and gender mainstreaming in the implementation of the laws and policies.

Section 2 of this report is structured according to the framework. Section 2.1 analyzes the Constitution of Lao PDR and the national laws that promote gender equality and prohibit discrimination. Given the number of laws related to climate change and disaster risk, this thematic area has been divided and section 2.2 covers laws related to disaster risk management while laws related to climate change and environmental management are reviewed in section 2.3. As agriculture is central to livelihoods in the Lao PDR and is highly vulnerable to the impacts of hazards and

---

[13]   UN General Assembly. 1979. Convention on the Elimination of All Forms of Discrimination Against Women. Adopted 18 December. *Treaty Series.* 1249.

[14]   UN Women Asia and the Pacific. N.d. *Lao PDR.*

[15]   CEDAW. 2018. *General Recommendation No.37 on Gender-Related Dimensions of Disaster Risk Reduction in the Context of Climate Change (CEDAW/C/GC/37).* para. 8. New York: CEDAW.

[16]   This report adopts CEDAW's recommended minimum standards of disaggregated data. This suggests that data be disaggregated by sex, age, disability, ethnicity, and geographical location as much as possible. The term "sex-disaggregated data" is used for brevity throughout this report.

[17]   ADB. 2021. *Gender-Inclusive Legislative Framework and Laws to Strengthen Women's Resilience to Climate Change and Disaster Risk.* Manila.

Figure 1. A National Good Practice Legislative Framework for Strengthening Women's Resilience to Climate Change and Disasters

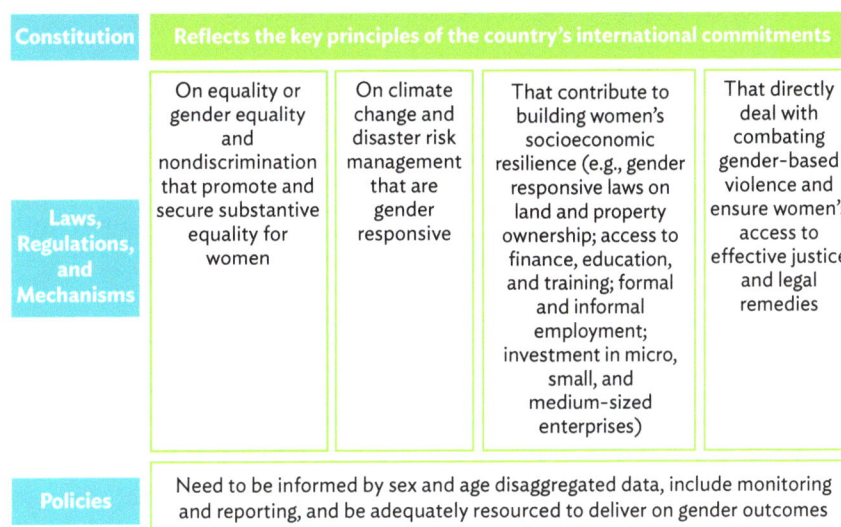

Constitution	Reflects the key principles of the country's international commitments			
Laws, Regulations, and Mechanisms	On equality or gender equality and nondiscrimination that promote and secure substantive equality for women	On climate change and disaster risk management that are gender responsive	That contribute to building women's socioeconomic resilience (e.g., gender responsive laws on land and property ownership; access to finance, education, and training; formal and informal employment; investment in micro, small, and medium-sized enterprises)	That directly deal with combating gender-based violence and ensure women's access to effective justice and legal remedies
Policies	Need to be informed by sex and age disaggregated data, include monitoring and reporting, and be adequately resourced to deliver on gender outcomes			

Source: ADB. 2021. *Gender-Inclusive Legislative Framework and Laws to Strengthen Women's Resilience to Climate Change and Disaster Risk*. Manila.

climate change, a gender analysis of laws related to agriculture is presented in section 2.4. Finally, national laws and policies that contribute to building women's socioeconomic resilience are analyzed and presented in section 2.5. It is noted that the full spectrum of laws and policies as set out in the framework cannot be addressed in this report. However, some of these thematic issues are touched upon throughout the analysis.

1.4 Methodology

The primary methodology in preparing the report was desk-based research and gender analysis of selected laws and policies, supplemented by country consultations, national workshops, and feedback on a draft report. Using the framework developed, a selection of laws and policies from the Lao PDR were gender analyzed.

The gender analysis encompassed the following steps:

(i)   review the overall purpose of the law or policy;

(ii)   assess the relevance of the instrument to gender, its content, and its potential impact upon women, especially women's resilience;

(iii) look at the language used and determine whether it makes distinctions based on sex, gender roles, or gender stereotypes;

(iv) assess laws or policies on a continuum of gender integration from lowest to highest: from gender negative, gender neutral, gender sensitive, gender responsive, to gender positive and/or transformative. Then classify them into three recurring categories: gender responsive, gender sensitive, or not yet gender mainstreamed, with some additional specific references to gender positive and/or transformative examples; and

(v)   make recommendations, and/or highlight any good practices in the law or policy to enhance the commitment to gender equality through laws and policies which contribute to promoting women's resilience in climate change and disaster risk management.

The purpose of classifying laws and policies on a continuum is to identify where gaps exist and where best practice examples can be highlighted. The continuum is adapted from the UN Women Training Centre[18] and WHO 2012 Mainstreaming Gender in Health Adaptation to Climate Change Programmes.[19] This analysis applies a three-point scale (color coded throughout) using authoritative international terminology:

(i)   **Gender responsive (green):** Pays attention to specific needs of women and men and intentionally uses gender considerations to affect the design, implementation, and results of legislation, policies, and programs.[20]

(ii) **Gender sensitive (yellow):** Considers gender norms, roles, and relations taking into account sociocultural factors, but does not actively address gender inequalities.[21]

(iii) **Not yet gender mainstreamed (orange):** No attention to gender equality issues have been made, which may result in a gender neutral or a gender negative outcome.

It is important to note that where possible, the report refers to gender and gender-responsiveness as much as possible rather than to women only. This recognizes that laws, policies, programs, and actions affect both men and women and that sometimes gender roles can disadvantage women and girls and sometimes disadvantage men and boys, often in different ways. However, based on CEDAW GR37 and the gender-based vulnerabilities and risks to the realization of women's rights from climate and disaster risk, the report focuses specifically on women's resilience. This is in alignment with the pursuit of gender equality and empowerment of women and girls under Sustainable Development Goal 5 (SDG5) and was articulated in the *Asia-Pacific Declaration on Advancing Equality and the Women's Empowerment: Beijing+25 Review.*[22] This report therefore primarily addresses how laws, policies, and gender mainstreaming can enhance women's resilience to these risks in the Lao PDR.

1.5 Gender, Climate Change, and Disaster Profile of the Lao People's Democratic Republic

The following profile highlights key climate hazards and disaster risks in the Lao PDR and presents the socioeconomic profile of women in the country as it relates to the identified risks.

Climate and disaster risk. The Lao PDR faces environmental management challenges that are amplified by climate change. While the country is not as highly exposed to natural hazards as some others in the Association of Southeast Asian Nations region, the limited economic resources of the Lao PDR create challenges for disaster management, increasing disaster risk for both the population and economy.[23] The vast majority of the Lao PDR terrain is mountainous, and the mountains in its northern, eastern, and southern regions create a significant natural buffer to storms, while the remaining terrain is mainly flat floodplains along the Mekong River, which are exposed to regular flooding.[24] The Lao PDR has a tropical climate, with average temperatures at 20°C in its plateaus and mountainous areas, and 25°C–27°C in its plains (footnote 26). The Lao PDR has a monsoon season from May to mid-October, followed by a dry season from mid-October to April (footnote 26).

[18]   UN Women Training Centre. 2017. *Gender Equality Glossary.* New York.

[19]   WHO. 2012. *Mainstreaming Gender in Health Adaptation to Climate Change Programmes.* Table 1. p. 10. Geneva.

[20]   UNICEF. 2017. *Gender Equality Glossary of Terms and Concepts.* Kathmandu.

[21]   WHO. 2012. *Mainstreaming Gender in Health Adaptation to Climate Change Programmes.* Geneva.

[22]   Economic and Social Commission for Asia and the Pacific (ESCAP). 2019. *Asia-Pacific Declaration on Advancing Gender Equality and Women's Empowerment: Beijing +25 Review.* Prepared for the Asia-Pacific Ministerial Conference on the Beijing+25 Review. Beijing. 27–29 November.

[23]   Kindernothilfe, Medico International, Oxfam, Plan International, Terre des hommes and Welthungerhilfe. 2020. *World Risk Report 2020 - Focus: Forced Displacement and Migration.* Berlin.

[24]   UN Development Programme (UNDP). N.d. *Lao PDR.* New York. (https://www.adaptation-undp.org/explore/south-eastern-asia/lao-peoples-democratic-republic).

The Lao PDR is already experiencing the adverse effects of climate change (Table 1). Economic losses from extreme weather and climate-related disasters increased during 2009–2019.[25] Climate change is projected to increase the severity of the most frequent and impactful natural hazards in the Lao PDR—floods, storms, and droughts—by causing longer hot and dry periods and an increase in average rainfall that is likely to cause more intense rainfall in the wet season.[26]

Table 1: An Overview of Key Climatic and Mixed Hazards of the Lao People's Democratic Republic Faces

Floods: These events are caused by tropical storms and monsoons and can also take the form of flash flooding, including damage to dams. They are the most frequent and destructive hazards for the Lao PDR and caused 37% of hazard-related deaths, 85% of hazard-related injuries, and 77% of recorded economic losses during 1990–2018. The low-lying floodplains of the Mekong River and its tributaries are the most exposed areas of the country to flooding. Floods cause the outbreak of diseases—including acute diarrheal disease, dengue fever, and malaria—and adversely impact rice production, with significant consequences for rural livelihoods and food security. Women are disproportionately affected by floods. For example, floods in 2018 increased women's workloads and the risk of experiencing GBV in temporary shelters and camps.[a]

Storms: Storms are strongest during the monsoon season and most adversely affect low-lying floodplain areas, including their production of key crops such as rice. During 1990–2018, storms were responsible for 10% of the country's recorded hazard-related economic losses. Climate change is predicted to exacerbate storms by increasing annual rainfall by an estimated 7% in the region.[b]

Droughts: Droughts affected 9% of the population during 1990–2018. Droughts can result in water shortages, which represent an emerging risk for the Lao PDR agriculture sector and a particular concern for subsistence farmers. Droughts impact health outcomes and hydroelectric power generation and can contribute to increases in pollution, forced migration, and the prevalence of diseases. The impacts of droughts are predicted to significantly worsen in the southern regions of Lao PDR in the coming years (footnote 30).

Landslides: These are often correlated with high precipitation due to floods and storms, and result in significant losses of lives, property, and agricultural production. Landslides threaten an estimated 5.24% of the country's terrain, mainly in the southeast and central regions which are characterized by steep topography and particular soil conditions.[c]

Earthquakes: These are a significant risk as a quarter of the Lao PDR is considered high-risk, and more than 30% is classified as a moderate hazard zone. However, no notable earthquake-related disasters have been reported in past years.[d]

Epidemics: The Lao PDR has experienced epidemics including tuberculosis, malaria, dengue fever, and—most recently—the coronavirus disease (COVID-19) pandemic. During 1990–2018, epidemics affected 8% of the Lao PDR population, causing 29% of hazard-related deaths and 13% of injuries. They also caused significant indirect or cascading economic impacts. The COVID-19 pandemic has disproportionately affected women, both in its economic impacts—which have particularly affected the informal sector wherein women are overrepresented—and through a "shadow pandemic" of GBV in many countries (footnote 32).[e]

Unexploded Ordnances (UXO): More than 2 million tons of bombs were dropped on the Lao PDR during the second Indochina war, making it one of the most bombed countries in the world. However, the Lao PDR National Committee for Rural Development and Poverty Eradication estimates that up to 30% of remaining ordnances have not exploded. Consequently, land in much of the country must be cleared before use, which prevents access to agricultural land and increases the cost of development. UXO kills and injures dozens of people each year.[f]

COVID-19 = coronavirus disease, GBV = gender-based violence, Lao PDR = Lao People's Democratic Republic.

Sources:
[a] UNDRR. 2019. *Disaster Risk Reduction in Lao PDR: Status Report 2019*. Bangkok; World Bank. 2019. *Post-Disaster Needs Assessment in Lao PDR: Helping Flood Recovery and Resilience Building*. Washington, DC; Government Lao PDR. 2019. *Post-Disaster Needs Assessment 2018 Floods, Lao PDR*. Vientiane; Government of Lao PDR, Ministry of Labor and Social Welfare (MLSW). 2020. *Lao-Di*. Vientiane.
[b] UNDRR. 2019. *Disaster Risk Reduction in Lao PDR: Status Report 2019*. Bangkok; Government of Lao PDR, Ministry of Labor and Social Welfare (MLSW). 2020. *Lao-Di*. Vientiane.
[c] Government of Lao PDR, National Disaster Management Committee. 2010. *National Risk Profile of Lao PDR November 2010*. Vientiane; UNDRR. 2019. *Disaster Risk Reduction in Lao PDR: Status Report 2019*. Bangkok.
[d] UNDRR. 2019. *Disaster Risk Reduction in Lao PDR: Status Report 2019*. Bangkok.
[e] UN Women. 2021. *The Shadow Pandemic: Violence against Women during COVID-19*; Government of Lao PDR, Ministry of Labor and Social Welfare (MLSW). 2020. *Lao-Di*. Vientiane.
[f] Government of Lao PDR, National Committee for Rural Development and Poverty Eradication: Lao National Unexploded Ordnance Programme. n.d. The UXO Problem. Vientiane; UNDP Lao PDR. n.d. Unexploded Ordnance (UXO).

---

[25] UNDRR. 2019. Disaster Risk Reduction in Lao PDR: Status Report 2019. Bangkok.
[26] World Bank Climate Change Knowledge Portal. N.d. Laos: Climate Data Projections (accessed 7 February 2020).

These hazards directly impact lives and livelihoods and are experienced differently by women and men. Yet, these differences are often not well understood due to the lack of both quantitative and qualitative sex-disaggregated data. This evidence is not widely and systematically collected in the Lao PDR, as in many countries in the Asian region. In absence of this data, a review of the Lao PDR socioeconomic profile can be used to understand the situation for women compared to men in the country and determine key gender-based inequalities and discrimination that exist and can affect women's capacity to build resilience.

Socioeconomic dimensions of gender and climate change and disaster risk management. In addition to the direct impacts of climate change and disasters, many indirect effects are relevant in the Lao PDR. These include migration, changes like work, and new opportunities that can open up with investment in areas such as the marketization of agriculture. Both direct and indirect impacts of climate change and hazards for women and men are determined by preexisting gender inequalities. A meta-analysis of reports on disasters in 141 countries found that gender differences in death rates were directly linked to women's economic and social rights; that in societies where women and men enjoyed equal rights there were no significant sex differences in the number of deaths.[27] The worst impacts on women from disasters and climate change—and the disadvantages that emerge in decision making by societies on adaptation—happen because women are already structurally disadvantaged by entrenched gender inequality, direct and indirect discrimination, and social and economic disadvantage. The most relevant socioeconomic factors for women in the Lao PDR are the levels of women in governance in 2021 (including Parliament, leadership, and decision-making positions), health status, education, the types of economic sectors where women work, employment and working conditions, ownership of land and assets, and the overarching impact of gender-based violence. These socioeconomic elements are discussed in the remainder of the profile for the Lao PDR.

Governance. In 1995, the United Nations Division of the Advancement of Women issued a report in which experts regarded 30% as being a critical minimum mass required for women as a group to exert a meaningful influence in legislative assemblies.[28] Data collected by IPU Parline in 2021 showed that the Lao PDR was 102 out of 188 countries with a 21.95% representation of women in *Sapha Heng Xat,* its national Parliament.[29] Women accounted for 31.5% of provincial assemblies in 2018 and 45% of civil servants in 2017.[30] However in 2018, women made up a very low proportion of village chiefs and deputy chiefs, other government decision making institutions, and members of disaster management committees at all levels (footnote 38).[31] The 2021 Global Gender Gap Index of the World Economic Forum categorized the political empowerment of women in the country as relatively positive due to improvements in women's representation in managerial and senior roles. The Lao PDR was placed 36 out of the 156 countries listed.[32]

Health. The Lao PDR has one of the highest rates of early marriage in the world—with one in four women aged 15–19 years old currently married—and the highest adolescent pregnancy in the region, with almost a quarter of girls aged 15–19 already having had a child.[33] The high adolescent birth rate causes an intergenerational cycle of malnutrition, with almost half of girls aged 15–19 suffering from anemia.[34] Chronic malnutrition is prevalent across all age groups in the Lao PDR, which also has a high prevalence of childhood stunting (44.2% of children), and

---

27   E. Neumayer and T. Plumper. 2007. The Gendered Nature of Natural Disasters: The Impact of Catastrophic Events on the Gender Gap in Life Expectancy, 1981–2002. *Annals of the American Association of Geographers.* 97, 3.

28   UN Division for the Advancement of Women. 2005. *Equal Participation of Women and Men in Decision-Making Processes, with Particular Emphasis on Political Participation and Leadership. Report of the Expert Group Meeting.* 24–27 October. Addis-Ababa.

29   Inter-Parliamentary Union (IPU). 2021. Monthly Ranking of Women in National Parliaments (accessed 20 June 2021).

30   Government of Lao PDR. 2018. *Lao People's Democratic Republic: Voluntary National Review on the Implementation of the 2030 Agenda for Sustainable Development.* Vientiane.

31   From the level of Deputy Director General up to Minister.

32   World Economic Forum. 2021. *Global Gender Gap Report 2021.* Cologny.

33   Government of Lao PDR. 2018. *Lao People's Democratic Republic: Voluntary National Review on the Implementation of the 2030 Agenda for Sustainable Development.* Vientiane; Government of Lao PDR, Statistics Bureau. 2017. *Statistical Yearbook 2016.* Vientiane.

34   Government of Lao PDR. 2018. *Lao People's Democratic Republic: Voluntary National Review on the Implementation of the 2030 Agenda for Sustainable Development.* Vientiane.

worse child health and nutrition outcomes than other countries in the mainland Southeast Asia region.[35] These health outcomes are influenced by a range of factors including poverty, food insecurity, and gender inequality.[36] While Lao PDR has significantly reduced mortality rates for infants (40 per thousand live births) and under-five-year-olds (46 per thousand live births), inequities remain. Children in the poorest quintile of households are nearly three times more likely to die than those in the highest quintile.[37] The Lao PDR also has the highest maternal mortality ratio of all Association of Southeast Asian Nations countries (footnote 45).

Disasters impact health outcomes in the Lao PDR as storms, flooding, and droughts impact agricultural production and adversely impact food security.[38] Outbreaks of diseases such as diarrheal disease, malaria, and typhoid fever are prevalent in the Lao PDR partly due to these hazards, and the incidence of tuberculosis is the highest in the region. Major disasters—such as typhoon Haima in 2011, or the 2018 floods—worsen health outcomes due to damage to health-care facilities and destruction of livelihoods.[39]

Education. Girls and boys are enrolled equally in early childhood education in the Lao PDR and the country has nearly achieved gender parity at the primary school level.[40] However, a lower proportion of girls attend each stage of secondary school, with 91 girls attending upper secondary for every 100 boys (footnote 49). In 2017, 41.8% of girls aged 15–17 were not in school (footnote 49).[41] Among girls, access to education is uneven. Girls—especially those from ethnic minority and poorer families—leave school at higher levels than boys at every school level, and girls from the lowest wealth quintile are significantly underrepresented in upper secondary school.[42] There are also disparities in educational provision between rural and urban areas.[43]

Stark gender inequities exist for literacy at all levels, although these are more pronounced among older age groups.[44] While in 2015 female adult literacy rate increased to 79%, the male literacy rate was still much higher at 90%.[45] These gender differences in educational attainment and literacy affect women's employment opportunities.[46]

Economic sectors. In 2018, three major sectors accounted for the gross domestic product (GDP) of the Lao PDR: services (46.8%), industry (35.5%), and agriculture (17.7%).[47] However, the highest numbers of workers were employed in (i) agriculture, forestry, and fishing; (ii) wholesale and retail trade; then (iii) public administration and defense. More than one-third of employed men and women work in agriculture. Besides agriculture, employed women were more likely to be in manufacturing, while employed men were more likely to be in public administration and defense.[48] In both urban and rural areas, women were more likely to be managers and professionals than men (footnote 57). Despite their contribution to GDP and the economy as a whole, electricity and gas comprise only 0.7% of employment, and mining only 0.5%, reflecting the resource-driven, capital-intensive nature of economic growth of the Lao PDR during 2017–2020.[49]

---

[35] UNDRR. 2019. *Disaster Risk Reduction in Lao PDR: Status Report 2019*. Bangkok; Y. Kamiya et al. 2018. Mothers' Autonomy and Childhood Stunting Evidence from Semi-Urban Communities in Lao PDR. *BMC Women's Health*. 18, 70.

[36] Y. Kamiya et al. 2018. Mothers' Autonomy and Childhood Stunting Evidence from Semi-Urban Communities in Lao PDR. *BMC Women's Health*. 18, 70.

[37] UNICEF Laos. 2020. *The Situation of Children and Women of Lao People's Democratic Republic*. Vientiane.

[38] UNDRR. 2019. *Disaster Risk Reduction in Lao PDR: Status Report 2019*. Bangkok.

[39] Government of Lao PDR. 2018. *Post-Disaster Needs Assessment (PDNA) 2018 Floods Lao PDR*. Vientiane.

[40] UNICEF Laos. 2020. *The Situation of Children and Women of Lao People's Democratic Republic*. Vientiane.

[41] Government of Lao PDR. 2017. Lao Social Indicator Survey, cited in: Government of Lao PDR. 2018. *Lao People's Democratic Republic: Voluntary National Review on the Implementation of the 2030 Agenda for Sustainable Development*. Vientiane.

[42] UNICEF Laos. 2020. *The Situation of Children and Women of Lao People's Democratic Republic*. Vientiane.

[43] Government of Lao PDR, Statistics Bureau. 2017. Statistical Yearbook 2016. Vientiane

[44] UNICEF Laos. 2020. *The Situation of Children and Women of Lao People's Democratic Republic*. Vientiane.

[45] Government of Lao PDR. 2018. *Lao People's Democratic Republic: Voluntary National Review on the Implementation of the 2030 Agenda for Sustainable Development*. Vientiane.

[46] Government of Lao PDR, Ministry of Planning and Investment and Statistics Bureau. 2018. *Lao PDR Labour Force Survey 2017*. Vientiane.

[47] ADB. 2021. *Key Indicator Data Base Lao PDR* (accessed 2 June 2021).

[48] Government of Lao PDR, Ministry of Planning and Investment and Statistics Bureau. 2018. *Lao PDR Labour Force Survey 2017*. Vientiane.

[49] UNICEF Laos. 2020. *The Situation of Children and Women of Lao People's Democratic Republic*. Vientiane.

Employment and working conditions. Women and men face different obstacles in employment because cultural norms and behaviors perpetuate gender divisions of labor, which in turn affects decent work for women. The obstacles for women include discrimination against them in employment and working conditions—including sexual harassment in the workplace and lower remuneration—compared to men, resulting in a gender wage gap. The labor force participation rate of women in the Lao PDR in 2018 was 36.5%—lower than that of men (45.2%)—demonstrating that women have fewer opportunities than men to be engaged in productive employment.[50] For both men and women, labor force participation rates were higher in urban areas than rural areas. There is a notable gender wage gap, with female employees earning on average 20% less than men (footnote 59).

Many workers in the informal sector are "vulnerable," meaning that they earn low incomes, experience poor working conditions, and have limited access to social protection and workplace representation.[51] Despite economic growth in recent decades, many working-age people in the Lao PDR are engaged in subsistence-level activities (footnote 60). Restoring livelihoods in subsistence-level and insecure employment after disasters can be challenging. Also, the majority of unpaid family workers are women, largely due to gender roles and limited educational and productive opportunities.[52] In 2015, 61% of women workers were unpaid family workers, compared to 26% of men.[53]

Workplace sexual harassment has serious impacts on women's health and well-being and their capacity to remain in secure long-term employment. There is a lack of official data and information or research about workplace sexual harassment in the Lao PDR, and "sexual harassment" is not explicitly defined and prohibited in law. The Law on Labor 2014 allows a worker to end an employment contract in the event of sexual harassment but does not protect workers from all forms of sexual harassment in employment or provide for adequate remedies or sanctions.[54]

Land, inheritance, and housing. Land, inheritance, and housing are vital components of women's economic resilience to disasters and the effects of climate change. In law, women, men, boys, and girls have equal inheritance rights, but in practice, unequal customary traditions often prevail (discussed in section 2.5.3). Under Article 17 of the Constitution of Lao PDR, men and women have equal property rights, including land.[55] However, in practice, women are often not registered on land titles, and in the case of jointly owned marital property, usually only husbands are registered on the title to land.[56] Women's lack of formal title to marital land and housing often negatively impacts their access to compensation for loss and restoration of housing and land in disasters.

Gender-based violence (GBV). Research in 2016 highlighted the high incidence and prevalence of GBV in the Lao PDR.[57] The 2014 Lao National Survey on Women's Health and Life Experiences found that almost one in three ever-partnered women reported at least one type of physical, sexual, or emotional violence by their partner.[58] GBV is an intergenerational phenomenon, as the survey found that one in 10 women had experienced sexual abuse during childhood, and a 2015 study on violence against children also found that more than a third of girls are subjected to some form of violence (footnote 67).[59]

---

[50] Government of Lao PDR, Ministry of Planning and Investment and Statistics Bureau. 2018. *Lao PDR Labour Force Survey 2017*. Vientiane.
[51] UNICEF Laos. 2020. *The Situation of Children and Women of Lao People's Democratic Republic*. Vientiane.
[52] Government of Lao PDR, Ministry of Planning and Investment and Statistics Bureau. 2018. *Lao PDR Labour Force Survey 2017*. Vientiane.
[53] Government of Lao PDR. 2018. *Lao People's Democratic Republic: Voluntary National Review on the Implementation of the 2030 Agenda for Sustainable Development*. Vientiane.
[54] Government of Lao PDR. 2014. *Labor Law (Amended)*. [Unofficial Translation]. Vientiane.
[55] Government of Lao PDR. 1991. *Constitution of the Lao People's Democratic Republic 1991 (Rev. 2003)*. Article 17. Vientiane.
[56] Government of Lao PDR, LWU. 2018. *Lao PDR Gender Profile*. Vientiane.
[57] Government of Lao PDR, National Commission for the Advancement of Women. 2016. *Lao National Survey on Women's Health and Life Experiences 2014*. Vientiane; Government of Lao PDR, *National Commission for Mothers and Children, Lao Statistics Bureau and UNICEF Lao PDR.* 2016. *National Violence against Children Survey in Lao PDR*. Preliminary Report. Vientiane.
[58] Government of Lao PDR, National Commission for the Advancement of Women. 2016. *Lao National Survey on Women's Health and Life Experiences 2014*. Vientiane.
[59] Government of Lao PDR, National Commission for Mothers and Children, Lao Statistics Bureau, and UNICEF Lao PDR. 2016. *National Violence against Children Survey in Lao PDR*. Preliminary Report. Vientiane.

GBV not only causes a personal toll on women victims/survivors, but also significant socioeconomic impacts on women generally and the community. It affects women's resilience to the impacts of climate change and disasters, increasing health risks and potentially preventing them from accessing economic opportunities or attending regular work. Prevention and mitigation of GBV also need to be included in disaster response planning for temporary shelters and ongoing access for affected communities. A 2018 report by the International Federation of Red Cross and Red Crescent Societies recommended that the Lao PDR strengthen local capacity to prevent and respond to GBV during and after disasters by investing in the training of all disaster responders.

This brief country profile presents the context of women's inequality and discrimination in the Lao PDR, which poses serious threats to the socioeconomic situation of women and their ability to build resilience to climate and disaster risks. While this report recognizes the many successes in advancing gender equality in the Lao PDR, it also analyzes the gaps and needs that are not yet being addressed to build women's resilience.

2 Laws, Policies, and Institutions Supporting Women's Resilience to Climate Change and Disasters

This section of the report presents the results of the application of the framework. Each subsection includes a brief description of the links between gender equality and the relevant thematic area, an overview of the key laws, policies, and institutions, followed by the results and the gender analysis summary.

2.1 National Structure for Gender Equality and Nondiscrimination

A good national structure to promote gender equality and prevent discrimination against women should have laws that guarantee the fundamental rights for women. Policies should further amplify legal provisions and implement legislative guarantees. These fundamental rights should preferably be expressed in a constitution, as this supreme law sets the platform for all laws. It emphasizes their importance and provides a sound basis for interpreting all other legislation. The essential concepts of equality and discrimination need to be visible in laws (Box 1).

Box 1: The Essential Concepts of Equality and Discrimination

The fundamental rights of equality and discrimination—in relation to women—include the concepts of *formal equality* (equal treatment of women and men); *substantive equality* (equality of outcome or results for women and men); promotion of equality (taking positive steps to achieve substantive equality); prohibiting *sex discrimination* both *direct discrimination* (laws, provisions or requirements, which expressly disadvantage women in comparison to men); and *indirect discrimination* (neutral laws, provisions or requirements, which have the effect of disadvantaging women in comparison to men); *exceptions* to discrimination (making allowances for biological difference such as pregnancy); *exemptions* from discrimination (where discriminating characteristics are inherent requirements for a particular job); and *temporary special measures* (taking positive measures to redress historical disadvantages to women and bring about substantive equality with men). These essential concepts of equality and discrimination need to be set out in legislation with a sufficient degree of specificity and detail, to enable them to be applied and enforced.

For more information and sources see Glossary.

The *National Good Practice Legislative Framework on Strengthening Women's Resilience to Climate Change and Disasters* presented in section 1.3 (Figure 1) presents five key areas for analysis. Two are addressed in this section: (i) the Constitution of Lao PDR, and (ii) national laws that prohibit gender discrimination and promote substantive equality.

2.1.1 Overview of Laws, Policies, and Institutions Related to Promoting Gender Equality and Nondiscrimination

The Constitution of Lao PDR 1991 (amended in 2003 and revised in 2015) provides for an independent democratic republic, with democratic elections via universal equal direct suffrage and secret ballot, and the Lao People's Revolutionary Party as the country's leading party.[60] The legislature is made up of the National Assembly and the permanent National Assembly Standing Committee.[61] The President of the Lao PDR—elected by the National Assembly—represents the country and appoints the Prime Minister, Vice President, ministers, and other officials with the agreement of the National Assembly. The President also affirms or denies laws adopted by the National Assembly (Article 60). The most powerful position is the General Secretary of the Lao People's Revolutionary Party, who is selected by the Party Committee and serves as the commander-in-chief of the Lao People's Armed Forces. The Lao Front for National Construction, the Lao Veterans Federation, the Lao Federation of Trade Unions, the Lao People's Revolutionary Youth Union, and the Lao Women's Union (LWU) are tasked with developing the country's right to self-determination. They have the right to monitor the activities of the National Assembly, the Local People's Assemblies, and members of such assemblies (Article 4).

In 2021, the Lao PDR had only 21.95% representation of women in Parliament. These rates have been low for some years, although they are one of the highest in Southeast Asia.[62] The Lao PDR does not have gender quotas in *Sapha Heng Xat*, its national Parliament.[63] Quotas are one way to achieve gender parity in the most important political body in the country, which countries including Nepal[64] and Uganda have done successfully.[65] The international consensus is that quotas in legislation should be a minimum of 30% for one gender, which almost 30% of countries were achieving as of 2012.[66] The gender composition of Parliament is a factor that can affect the gender responsiveness of the lawmaking process and the content of laws, including those relating to environmental management, climate change, and disaster protection.

The most important laws on the process of making laws and their content are the Law on Making Legislation 2012 and the Law on Gender Equality 2019 (LGE), which have been gender analyzed and the summary of findings presented in section 2.1.3. The Law on Making Legislation 2012 requires wide national and provincial consultations before laws are finalized and enables the Women's Caucus of the National Assembly to comment on laws concerning women before finalization.[67] It also provides that if legislation is inconsistent with the provisions of related treaties, then the provisions of treaties shall prevail and national legislation be amended (Articles 7[2] and 9).[68] The LGE establishes the principles, regulations, and measures to mainstream gender throughout laws and policies in all sectors (Article 1). It defines and guarantees gender equality (Article 2; Chapter 2, Articles 26–31) and gender mainstreaming (Article 3[2]), and outlines important provisions amounting to temporary special measures, i.e., taking positive measures to redress historical disadvantages to women and create

---

60   Government of Lao PDR. 1991. *Constitution of the Lao People's Democratic Republic 1991 (Rev. 2003)*. Articles 3, 4. Vientiane.

61   Government of Lao PDR. 1991. *Constitution of the Lao People's Democratic Republic 1991 (Rev. 2003)*. Articles 1, 52, 53(6)–(8), 56, 66, 76–77. Vientiane.

62   IPU. 2021. Monthly Ranking of Women in National Parliaments (accessed 20 June 2021); OECD. 2019. *Government at a Glance Southeast Asia 2019: Country Fact Sheet Lao PDR*. Paris.

63   OECD. 2019. *Government at a Glance Southeast Asia 2019: Country Fact Sheet Lao PDR*. Paris.

64   The Constitution of Nepal 2015 requires that at least one third of total members elected from each political party must be women. As of 1 March 2020, there were 32.73% of women in the lower house and 38.67% in the upper house. IPU. 2020. Percentage of Women in National Parliaments: 2020 (accessed on 30 May 2020). Geneva.

65   The Constitution of the Republic of Uganda 1995 (amended 2005). Articles 78(1)(b), 178 (2)(b), 180(2)(b) requires one third representation of women. As of 1 March there are is 34.86% of women in Parliament. IPU. 2020. *Percentage of Women in National Parliaments*: 2020 (accessed on 30 May 2020). Geneva.

66   IPU. 2020. *Percentage of Women in National Parliaments: 2020* (accessed on 30 May 2020). Geneva.

67   Government of Lao PDR. 2012. *Law on Making Legislation*. Vientiane.

68   See also Government of Lao PDR. 2009. *Presidential Ordinance on Conclusion, Accession and Implementation of Treaties 2009*. Articles 2 and 35, cited in the *Human Rights Committee Consideration of reports submitted by States parties under article 40 of the Covenant pursuant to the optional reporting procedure Initial reports of States parties due in 2010 Lao People's Democratic Republic*. Vientiane; Government of Lao PDR. 2012. *Law on Making Legislation*. Vientiane.

substantive equality with men (Chapter 1, Article 24).[69] The key policy document guiding the promotion of gender equality and elimination of discrimination is the National Action Plan on Gender Equality 2021–2025 (NAPGE). Its goals are to promote gender equality, raise public awareness, develop a gender responsive database, develop national policies and legislation that commit to international agreements on women's rights to which the Lao PDR is a party, and strengthen the structure and personnel of gender equality institutions.[70] The NAPGE is designed to implement the principles of the LGE, and both are overseen by the National Commission for the Advancement of Women, Mothers, and Children (NCAWMC).

The key institutions for promoting gender equality and preventing discrimination against women are the LWU, the NCAWMC, and the Women's Parliamentary Caucus. The LWU is a mass organization established in 1955 with a total membership of over 1 million. It has a mandate for women's advancement under the Constitution (Article 7) and a mandate under the Law of the Lao Women's Union 2013 to represent and advocate for the rights of women and children (Article 8).[71] This mandate is further affirmed in the Law on Development and Protection of Women 2004 (Article 4)[72] and the Law on Preventing and Combatting Violence against Women and Children 2014 (Article 62).[73] Since 1997, the LWU has run Gender Resource Information and Development (GRID) centers, which develop key gender tools and training materials and conduct gender analysis workshops.

The NCAWMC is responsible for promoting gender equality and protecting the rights of children. It was formed in March 2018 through a merger of the National Commission for the Advancement of Women and the National Commission for Mother and Child and has since been incorporated into the LWU. The deputy prime minister is the chairperson, and the president of the LWU is the vice chairperson of the NCAWMC. The NCAWMC serves as the focal point for monitoring and implementing policies relating to gender equality and children's rights, as well as treaties such as the CEDAW Convention and the Convention on the Rights of the Child. The Women's Parliamentary Caucus was established by the National Assembly in 2010 to support gender mainstreaming in legislation, review laws related to women and children, and monitor their implementation.[74] The caucus is formally open to male members of Parliament but is comprised only of women members of Parliament, although many men parliamentarians support its work.[75]

2.1.2 The Constitution of the Lao PDR

The Constitution sets out the fundamental rights and obligations of its citizens in Chapter IV. There are four provisions with particular importance to supporting women's equality, empowerment, and resilience to climate change and disaster risk. The Constitution:

(i)   requires the state to acknowledge, respect, protect and guarantee the human rights of its citizens following its laws (Article 34);

(ii)   guarantees the equality of citizens before the law "irrespective of their gender, social status, education, beliefs, and ethnic group" (Article 35);

(iii) stipulates that "Citizens of both genders enjoy equal rights in the political, economic, cultural and social fields and in family affairs" (Article 37); and

(iv)   requires the state to promote women's and children's rights, including education, health, and work in skilled labor (Articles 22–30).[76]

---

69   Government of Lao PDR. 2019. *Law on Gender Equality*. [Unofficial Translation]. Vientiane.
70   Government of Lao PDR. 2021. *National Action Plan on Gender Equality (2021–2025)*. [Unofficial Translation]. Vientiane.
71   Government of Lao PDR. 2013. *Law of the Lao Women's Union*. Vientiane.
72   Government of Lao PDR. 2004. *Law on Development and Protection of Women*. Vientiane.
73   Government of Lao PDR. 2014. *Law on Preventing and Combatting Violence against Women and Children*. Vientiane.
74   CEDAW. 2017. *Consideration of Reports Submitted by States Parties Under Article 18 Of the Convention: Combined Eighth and Ninth Periodic Reports of States Parties Due In 2014: Lao People's Democratic Republic*. CEDAW/C/LAO/8–9. 3 August.
75   IPU Parline. 2021. *Lao People's Democratic Republic* (accessed 29 June 2021).
76   Government of Lao PDR. 1991. *Constitution of the Lao People's Democratic Republic 1991 (Rev. 2003)*. Vientiane.

The Constitution does not refer to the essential concepts of equality and discrimination, except by providing for "formal equality"—or equal treatment—in Articles 34 and 35. However, formal equality does not meet the standard of equality required by the CEDAW Convention—substantive equality—which refers to equal outcomes or results. The LGE fills some—but not all—gaps on equality and discrimination in the Constitution. Additionally, the Law on Preventing and Combatting Violence against Women and Children 2014 provides a more detailed definition of "discrimination against women" (Article 4, Paragraph 14). The Constitution provides for the formal equality of citizens, creating a foundation for other laws and policies to include the principles of substantive equality and nondiscrimination.

2.1.3 Gender Analysis Summary of Key Laws and Policies on Gender Equality and Nondiscrimination

A gender analysis was conducted of the key laws and policies to promote gender equality and prevent discrimination (Table 2). The color coded system is used to categorize the laws and policies and demonstrates the state of gender mainstreaming as of 2021.

Table 2: Summary of the Gender Equality and Nondiscrimination Framework

Law/Policy	Summary of Gender References
Law on Gender Equality 2019 (LGE)	It references mainstreaming gender in all areas of work (Article 5[4], 22[3]) and includes gender responsive provisions on overcoming cultural beliefs that inhibit women's advancement (Articles 18, 30[4] and 34). However, it does not provide for substantive equality, nor define and prohibit both direct and indirect discrimination according to international standards (CEDAW).
National Action Plan on Gender Equality (2021–2025) (NAPGE)	There are aspirational targets for capacity-building on gender equality for National Assembly members. There are also positive targets to promote equality and improve women's resilience to disasters and increase the participation of women in climate change and disaster risk reduction.
Law on Making Legislation 2012	It requires wide national and provincial consultations and enables the Women's Caucus to comment on laws before finalization. It does not mention the concepts of equality or nondiscrimination.

CEDAW = Convention on the Elimination of All Forms of Discrimination Against Women.
Note: Color coding: gender responsive (green), gender sensitive (yellow), not yet gender mainstreamed (orange).
Source: Asian Development Bank.

The LGE is categorized gender responsive. The law incorporates important principles and goals that are broad and aspirational and contains some gender responsive provisions. It also contains provisions amounting to temporary special measures—or positive measures to redress historical disadvantages to women and produce substantive equality with men (Article 24)—although these are described in general terms. However, the LGE does not fully comply with the CEDAW Convention in several critical ways. The law does not include a definition or dedicated provision on either direct or indirect discrimination; provide sufficient clarity on the nature of gender discrimination; adequately cover the range of actions that amount to gender discrimination; or reference the effects of gender discrimination. All of these are required in the CEDAW Convention.[77]

The LGE does not include provisions on complaints procedures and to be effective in practice, the law requires the development of further regulations or other legal mechanisms and procedures. Women can seek remedies for adverse discrimination under the Penal Code, which criminalizes gender discrimination, with a penalty of 1 to 3 years imprisonment and a fine.[78] However, not all discrimination may be of sufficient seriousness to warrant a criminal response with a criminal burden of proof.

---

[77] UN General Assembly. 1979. Convention on the Elimination of All Forms of Discrimination Against Women. Adopted 18 December. *Treaty Series*. 1249. pp. 13.
[78] Government of Lao PDR. 2017. *Penal Code 2017*. Article 179. Vientiane.

The NAPGE is ambitious and covers a broad spectrum of gender responsive targets and priority activities. These include (i) public awareness campaigns in communities to eradicate harmful traditional practices that discriminate against women (Outcome 1); (ii) conducting awareness raising among National Assembly members (Outcome 1); and (iii) promoting gender equality by introducing positive measures across a broad range of activities including quotas for women in leadership roles in climate change, emergency response and disaster risk reduction and training for relevant actors in the justice system of particular relevance to GBV (Outcome 2).[79] The NAPGE also supports gender mainstreaming throughout all sectors as part of implementing the LGE. For example, Output 3.1 is that 80% of all sectors integrate gender equality into their work. The NAPGE also includes targets for strengthening the organizational structure of the NCAWMC and the capacity of its staff (Outcomes 4.1 and 4.2), which are directly linked to the LGE (Articles 35–40). For effective implementation of the NAPGE, NCAWMC will need to conduct assessments and develop more detailed action plans for each set of targets and establish processes for making complaints and determining grievances.

While the Law on Making Legislation 2012 enables the Women's Caucus to comment on laws before they are finalized, it does not include gender-specific criteria for assessing the impacts of the proposed laws.[80] It also does not include the essential concepts of equality and nondiscrimination. Therefore, it is categorized not yet gender mainstreamed.

The Lao PDR has some good precedents in its national framework on gender equality, of which the Constitution, the LGE, and the NAPGE are the most important legal and policy instruments. If implemented effectively together, they provide a solid foundation for gender mainstreaming in all laws and policies.

2.2 Gender and Disaster Risk Management

Disasters can affect men and women differently depending on levels of gender inequality, as well as gender roles in work allocation and family caring responsibilities. With women in the Lao PDR overrepresented in the informal sector, having lower wages in the formal sector, and having less access to land and housing, they may also suffer greater relative economic losses and longer recovery times if they lose their homes or possessions. This can also increase their unpaid workload of home and caring duties following disasters. It is important to look at gender roles within community and family structures to understand whether special measures are needed to address gender-based vulnerabilities and the needs of women or men in disasters. Gender analysis that examines gender roles and responsibilities and socioeconomic status in normal times plays an important role in disaster risk management and should inform law and policy-related decision making.

2.2.1 Overview of Key Laws, Policies, and Institutions Related to the Disaster Risk Management System

The main law in the Lao PDR on DRR is the Disaster Management Law 2019 (DM Law), which replaced all previous decrees on committees for disaster management and disaster prevention and control.[81] The DM Law is administered by the Ministry of Labor and Social Welfare (MLSW), separately from a government decree on climate change, which is administered by the Ministry of Natural Resources and Environment (MoNRE) (discussed in section 2.3.2). The law establishes an institutional framework and resources for disaster risk governance, allocating responsibilities to cross-sector central, provincial, and district disaster management committees, all of which are

79   Government of Lao PDR. 2021. *National Action Plan on Gender Equality (2021–2025)*. [Unofficial Translation]. Vientiane.
80   Government of Lao PDR. 2012. *Law on Making Legislation*. Vientiane.
81   Government of Lao PDR. 2019. *Law on Disaster Management 2019*. Vientiane. Now replaced by the DM Law: Government of Lao PDR. 1999. *Decree on Establishment of National Disaster Management Committee 1999*. Vientiane.

supported by the labor and social welfare sector (Articles 52, 53, and 54). The DM Law also establishes Village Disaster Management Committees, comprising village leadership and members of the Village Elderly, Youth Unit, and Lao Women's Union (Article 57). These committees lead community disaster management activities, act as a focal point for relevant stakeholders, and support District Disaster Management Committees.

In terms of policies, the government is finalizing a National Disaster Risk Reduction Strategy 2021–2030 (NDRRS), which will establish the framework for a 5-year national action plan on DRR and guide the Lao PDR overall strategy until 2030. Its implementation will coincide with the 9th National Socioeconomic Development Plan (2021–2025). The government has endeavored to mainstream DRR into the National Socioeconomic Development Plan through sector plans. Neither were available for analysis as of 2021 and as such are not included in section 2.2.2. While not official policy, it is worth noting that the Government of the Lao People's Democratic Republic has collaborated with international partners on community-based disaster risk reduction (CBDRR) to develop important guidance such as the CBDRR Manual and CBDRR Minimum Standards, which emphasize gender and women's equal participation as cross-cutting issues in disaster prevention and response.[82]

2.2.2 Gender Analysis Summary of Key Disaster Risk Management Law

A gender analysis was conducted of the Law on Disaster Management 2019 (DM Law) (Table 3). The color coded system is used to categorize the law and demonstrates the state of gender mainstreaming as of 2021. The table only contains the law as the draft strategy was not yet available for analysis.

Table 3: Summary of Gender Inclusion in Disaster Risk Management

Law/Policy	Summary of Gender References
Law on Disaster Management 2019 (DM Law)	It includes the principle of equality but not gender equality or nondiscrimination, although by referencing compliance with international conventions, it indirectly provides for CEDAW compliance (Article 5[1]). There are no principles or mechanisms to undertake gender analysis or move towards substantive gender equality, although it does provide for the participation of the LWU in Village Disaster Management Committees (Article 57). The DM Law recognizes one element of women's differentiated vulnerability by noting that pregnant women may require special support in disasters (Article 43[3]).

CEDAW = Convention on the Elimination of All Forms of Discrimination Against Women.
Note: Color coding: gender responsive (green), gender sensitive (yellow), not yet gender mainstreamed (orange).
Source: Asian Development Bank.

The DM Law is not gender mainstreamed, as it does not address gender as an issue or priority in disaster protection and assumes that men and women have the same types of needs and experience disasters in much the same way; it effectively assumes that there are no gender differences to consider. It does not include principles or mechanisms for gender analysis, which could inform gender responsive DRM measures such as prevention and response to GBV in disasters. Thus, the DM Law does not provide for gender analysis of disaster risk or impacts, nor gender balance in representation in institutions and decision-making roles. It includes the LWU in the new village committees only, in contrast to the previous Decree 75 on Disaster Prevention and Control, which mandated that central, provincial, and district DRM committees include an LWU representative.[83] It is worth noting that under the DM law, the government may assign additional representatives to committees if they have relevant expertise (Articles 52, 53,

---

[82]   Government of Lao PDR and ADPC. 2016. *Community-Based Disaster Risk Reduction (CBDRR) Manual in Lao PDR—Scaling-up Community-Based Disaster Risk Reduction in Lao PDR–Lao People's Democratic Republic (The)*. Vientiane; CARE et al. 2017. *Community Based Disaster Risk Reduction Minimum Standard [EN/LO]–Lao People's Democratic Republic (The)*. Vientiane.

[83]   Government of Lao PDR, Prime Minister. 2018. *Decree on Organization and Roles of the National Committee for Disaster Prevention and Control, Ref. no. 75/PM (repealed by Law on Disaster Management 2019)*. Vientiane.

and 54). LWU representatives could be appointed to committees on the basis that their expertise is relevant to all types of disasters, given the importance of gender as a factor in disaster impacts.

The DM Law does contain positive elements on which future gender responsive DRR strategies and plans can be built. These are:

(i)   A general reference to the Constitution, which enshrines formal equality, and compliance with international conventions, which includes the CEDAW Convention (Article 5[1]).

(ii) The principle of equality (Article 5[3]): "Ensure there is equality, fairness, transparency, openness, and accountability."

(iii) A recognition that "pregnant women, children, people with disabilities and the elderly" may require special services in disasters (Article 43[3]). This addresses one form of vulnerability that women may experience in disasters, although it is limited to one health issue and only to women's vulnerability, rather than resilience and contributions to DRM.

(iv) The inclusion of the LWU in village disaster management committees (Article 57), is an important form of women's representation in DRM at a community level.

These positive elements of the DM Law can be further elaborated in the NDRRS and 5-year national DRR action plans that the government will develop as part of implementing the DM Law and the NDRRS. These policy and planning initiatives are an opportunity to promote substantive gender equality in the implementation of the DM Law, such as conducting targeted capacity building for women civil servants and community leaders and promoting the meaningful participation of women in DRM committees at every level. They also offer opportunities to collaborate with other institutions to address the gender-specific needs of women in disaster contexts—such as the National Taskforce on the Prevention of Violence Against Women—on the important issues of GBV in disasters.

2.3 Gender, Climate Change, and Environmental Management

The impacts of climate change on the environment in the Lao PDR give added importance to environmental regulation beyond traditional concepts of protecting the environment and ecosystems. The law and policy framework must deal with the increasing incidence of floods and droughts, and their impacts on rural health forced migration and agricultural production, as well as major projects and industries such as hydropower production.[84] These events bring significant adverse consequences to food security and the agricultural economy, which may require adaptations in land use and changes to traditional rural livelihoods. This leads to greater competition for resources, and pressure to put shorter-term economic needs ahead of sustainable development. Well-managed change can provide opportunities for positive social change including improved gender equality in access to environmental resources.

Due to the wide-ranging impacts of climate change, many laws and policies are relevant to this topic, some of which are analyzed concerning the agriculture sector in section 2.4, and others regarding women's access to assets in section 2.5. Recent studies and small-scale assessments point to how gender roles and responsibilities result in differential impacts. Box 2 shows an example of gender roles in forestry, highlighting areas where laws and policies are needed to ensure gender equality in the pursuit of climate action and environmental management.

---

[84]   UNDRR. 2019. *Disaster Risk Reduction in Lao PDR: Status Report 2019.* Bangkok; and Government of Lao PDR, Ministry of Labor and Social Welfare (MLSW). 2020. *Lao-Di.* Vientiane.

Box 2: Gender Roles and Responsibilities in Forestry in Lao People's Democratic Republic

Men often control the most valuable forest resources, leaving women restricted to products with little commercial benefit. Men and women also have different roles in the forestry sector as well as different access to, and control over, forestlands. Traditionally, men hunt and collect timber while women have a greater role in non-timber forest products (NTFPs), such as cultivating vegetables and collecting roots, shoots, and firewood. Women often have intimate knowledge of forest resources and how they can be used. Women are also responsible for producing and marketing textiles and handicrafts that are frequently made from forest resources, and selling food and medicines obtained from the forest, commonly as part of micro and small businesses. Women also commonly use NTFPs to diversify their livelihoods, strengthening their resilience to climate change and disaster impacts. Any restrictions on access to land can significantly impact the livelihoods and resilience of women who rely on NTFPs.

Sources: Government of Lao PDR, LWU. 2018. *Lao PDR Gender Profile.* Vientiane; FAO. 2018. *Country Gender Assessment of Agriculture and the Rural Sector in Lao People's Democratic Republic.* Vientiane; Climate Investment Funds. 2017. *Gender and Sustainable Forest Management: Entry Points for Design and Implementation.* Washington, DC.

2.3.1 Overview of Laws, Policies, and Institutions Related to Climate Change and Environmental Management

The Lao PDR has three key legal instruments on climate change and environmental management. The Decree on Climate Change 2019 (CC Decree) is the country's first specific legal framework for its response to climate change. It establishes regulations for managing and monitoring climate change mitigation and adaptation measures towards the aim of sustainable development.[85] The Environmental Protection Law 2012 and the Decree on Environmental Impact Assessment 2019 (EIA Decree) provide the overarching framework for environmental protection most relevant to climate change. In the approval of projects, the Environmental Protection Law aims to "provide balance between social and natural environment, to sustain and to protect natural resources and public health; and contribute to national socioeconomic development and the reduction of global warming."[86] It endows affected communities with significant rights and requires a rigorous consultation process around initial environmental examinations, supported by the new EIA Decree. In terms of sector-specific laws, the Water and Water Resources Law (Revised 2017) is relevant to climate change and environmental management, and governs water rights and use to sustainably manage the Lao PDR water resources.[87]

The National Environment Committee (NEC)—a cross-sector committee chaired by the Deputy Prime Minister— is the top body in the Lao PDR for providing policy guidance on environmental management, including climate change.[88] Under the NEC, MoNRE is responsible for environmental policy and planning and MoNRE's Department of Climate Change (DCC) is the governing body for coordinating and implementing climate-related laws and policies.[89] The director general of DCC chairs the Technical Working Group on Climate Change, which coordinates climate change action between ministries and consults with the Green Climate Fund (GCF) on technical issues. The technical working group is comprised of technical representatives from a range of ministries—including the LWU—which promotes the representation of women within the national institutional framework.[90]

---

[85]   Government of Lao PDR. 2019. *Decree on Climate Change 2019 (Lao version).* Vientiane.

[86]   Government of Lao PDR. 2012. *Environmental Protection Law (Revised Version) 2012.* Article 1. Vientiane.

[87]   Government of Lao PDR. 2017. *Law on Water and Water Resources (Amended Version) 2017.* Vientiane.

[88]   GCF. 2019. *Lao PDR Country Programme.* Vientiane.

[89]   Government of Lao PDR. Capacity-Building Initiative for Transparency Global Coordination Platform. N.d. *Department of Climate Change of Lao PDR.*

[90]   GCF. 2019. *Lao PDR Country Programme.* Vientiane.

The key national policy on environmental management will be the new National Strategy on Climate Change (2021–2030), which is being designed by the DCC based on the CC Decree and international and regional commitments of the Lao PDR. As the strategy is still under development and the previous one is outdated, neither were gender analyzed for this report. The Lao PDR has several other policies relating to climate change as part of its reporting to the UNFCCC. These include its 2021 updated Nationally Determined Contribution (NDC), which addresses both climate change mitigation and adaptation;[91] its 2013 National Communication;[92] and its 2009 National Adaptation Program of Action (NAPA).[93]

2.3.2 Gender Analysis Summary of Key Climate and Environmental Laws and Policies

A gender analysis was conducted of the select laws and policies relevant to climate change and environmental protection (Table 4). The color coded system is used to categorize the laws and policies and demonstrates the state of gender mainstreaming as of 2021.

Table 4: Summary of Gender Inclusion in Climate and Environmental Laws and Policies

Law/Policy	Summary of Gender References
Decree on Climate Change 2019 (CC Decree)	It does not mention gender, gender roles, men, or women, either directly or indirectly nor the key concepts of equality and nondiscrimination. It focuses on the technical aspects of monitoring and data collection, not human impacts.
Environmental Protection Law (Rev. 2012)	It does not consider gender directly or indirectly. Stakeholder consultations and assessments are not required to consider gender equality or discrimination or make efforts to ensure women's participation. The law does not make provisions for women's participation in staffing or governance institutions.
Decree on Environmental Impact Assessments 2019 (EIA Decree)	It includes provisions on participatory consultations and assessments that mainstream gender, such as the requirement for project owners to collect baseline information on gender- and ethnicity-related issues (Article 13) and conduct assessments with management and monitoring plans relating to gender and ethnicity (Articles 22[7] and 36).
Water and Water Resources Law (Rev. 2017)	The law uses terms such as "user" and "household" and "family" as the people affected by and regulated by the law, without reference to gender, or women and girls.
Nationally Determined Contribution (NDC) 2021	This document does not include references to the principles of equality and nondiscrimination and includes only minor references to gender or women, most specifically in the Annex on Adaptation Health Adaptation Strategy (gender-equal participation in capacity building workshops and implementation plans on gender roles relating to climate change and health).
Second National Communication under UNFCCC 2013	It does not consider the gender dimensions of vulnerability to climate change impacts or address the differential impacts of climate change on men and women. Instead, it addresses the vulnerability of villages, the rural poor, and the agriculture sector.
National Adaptation Program of Action (NAPA) 2009	It does not reference gender, women and girls, or the principles of equality and nondiscrimination. It uses the household unit, or family, as the measure of poverty or impact or benefit, which precludes the collection of sex-disaggregated data and use of gender indicators for monitoring and evaluation.

Note: Color coding: gender responsive (green), gender sensitive (yellow), not yet gender mainstreamed (orange).
Source: Asian Development Bank.

[91]   Government of Lao PDR. 2021. *Nationally Determined Contribution*. Vientiane.
[92]   UNFCCC. N.d. *National Communication Submissions from Non-Annex I Parties*.
[93]   Government of Lao PDR. 2009. *National Adaptation Programme of Action to Climate Change*. Vientiane.

All but one of the laws and policies on climate change in the Lao PDR are not yet gender mainstreamed. Each of these laws and policies treats the scope of regulation as either neutral technical issues or social issues that are presumed to impact equally on all people. They do not include mandates or mechanisms for special measures to achieve substantive gender equality. Laws and policies on climate change in the Lao PDR do not provide any mechanisms for gender analysis of policies and plans, gender-sensitive processes, or mechanisms for public, community, and civil society participation, or gender mainstreaming in implementation.

The CC Decree focuses on the technical aspects of vulnerability—such as hazards—rather than the impacts of climate change on defined vulnerable groups. However, the decree requires vulnerability assessments and mapping, and the mainstreaming of such climate change knowledge into national and sector socioeconomic development plans and programs. This provides an avenue to address the social dimensions of climate change, such as the differential impacts, risks, and coping capacities of men and women. The CC Decree also does not promote a participatory model of action on climate change in which women's organizations can participate in risk assessments and adaptation planning and implementation. Consequently, if women are not already in formal leadership positions in government organizations, they have limited opportunities to participate in decision making relating to climate change under this law. Given that the NAPGE has clear targets on women's participation and leadership in climate change, it would be worthwhile to address these questions in any future review of the decree and the National Climate Change Strategy under development as of 2021.

While the Environmental Protection Law (Revised 2012) does not include gender considerations, there have been positive developments in its subsidiary laws and guidelines. The 2012 government environmental impact assessment guidelines introduced the use of gender-based data, gender considerations in community assessment studies, consultations, and socioeconomic criteria for EIAs.[94] While the guidelines are non-binding and do not give gender a high prominence, they provide sufficient guidance to underpin the practices of gender assessments, consultations with women, and gender mainstreaming into EIAs.

The EIA Decree is gender sensitive as it requires the collection of information and assessments relating to gender, but not the use of such assessments to equalize women's participation or improve their resilience. While the regulatory scope of national environmental management laws—such as the CC Decree—is broad, project and local area assessments occur in specific environments with specific populations. EIAs are therefore an opportunity to examine more closely any differential socioeconomic impacts of climate change on men and women, which can be leveraged to inform laws and policies. Although the EIA Decree does not specify that community consultations must seek the views of women, the stipulations for gender data and assessments essentially make this necessary to fulfill procedural requirements. When the guidelines are next reviewed, this could be made more explicit as a requirement for gender-inclusive consultation methods.

Apart from the EIA Decree, the Lao PDR laws and policies on climate change do not mandate the collection of sex-disaggregated data or the integration of gender in monitoring and evaluation. The international consensus is that sex-disaggregated data is essential for understanding the gendered impacts of climate change and for monitoring climate change laws and policies based on the experiences of men, women, boys, and girls.[95] These understandings can be used to design more effective gender responsive policies to build women's resilience to the impacts of climate change.

While the Water and Water Resources Law (Revised 2017) contains provisions for the protection of small-scale and household uses of water resources—which could be used to support and protect the livelihoods of women in small-scale agriculture and domestic labor—it does not provide a mechanism for monitoring or evaluating gender

---

94   Government of Lao PDR. 2012. *Environmental Impact Assessment Guidelines*. Vientiane.
95   CEDAW. 2018. *General Recommendation No. 37 On the Gender-Related Dimensions of Disaster Risk Reduction in the Context of Climate Change*. CEDAW/C/GC/37. 7 February.

impacts or needs. This inhibits the possibility of identifying the specific needs of women and designing solutions that promote substantive gender equality. Likewise, some Lao PDR NDC targets will likely yield significant benefits for women, but with the relatively limited integration of gender indicators into monitoring and evaluation, the needs of women and girls will mostly not be captured or used to inform future planning. The NDC does include two gender-related indicators on health only: (i) gender-equal participation in capacity building workshops; and (ii) implementation plans on gender roles relating to climate change and health (Annex 2), which are a positive step toward gender sensitivity. By using household data, the Lao PDR NAPA similarly precludes the analysis of gender impacts and benefits. These laws and policies were missed opportunities to integrate the gender considerations, particularly given the increasing global push to integrate gender and social inclusion into UNFCCC processes.

Overall, gender considerations have not been a significant part of climate change and environmental laws and policies in the Lao PDR. The membership of LWU in the Technical Working Group on Climate Change is a positive step toward increasing the participation of women and integration of gender concerns in the climate change institutional framework. However, their capacity to be an effective voice is necessarily limited by the lack of any specific gender criteria or targets in the law and policy framework on climate change. It is also worth noting that the the Lao PDR Green Climate Fund (GCF) Country Program 2019 has a significant influence over resource allocation for climate change mitigation and adaptation. Any related program activities under the GCF will be required to comply with the GCF Gender Policy and Action Plan, which establishes clear criteria for gender responsive climate action.[96] A more systematic approach to gender analysis and mainstreaming in the Lao PDR climate change laws and policies and their implementation—informed by sex-disaggregated qualitative and quantitative data—would better support women's resilience to climate change.

2.4 Gender and the Agriculture Sector

There is a direct link between climate change and agriculture, particularly in the Lao PDR where climate change is already affecting the production of staple crops such as rice. Climate change impacts—such as the increased incidence of floods, droughts, and storms—can force migration and threaten livelihoods and food security, particularly in rural agricultural communities.[97] This sector was chosen for particular analysis due to the status of the Lao PDR as a predominantly agrarian society, its vulnerability to the impacts of climate change, and its state of transition as the government encourages its rapid marketization, which provides uneven opportunities for different social groups.[98]

2.4.1 Overview of the Agriculture Sector

Agriculture is the largest source of productive employment in the Lao PDR, with approximately three-quarters of households engaged in agriculture.[99] However, the sector only accounts for 17.7% of GDP, reflecting the widespread nature of subsistence farming in the country in which 90% of rural households grow rice and only 30% grow additional crops.[100] Smallholders are responsible for most agricultural production.[101] Due to the complex topography of the Lao PDR, the country has over 40 unique livelihood groups.[102] For example, in lowlands, irrigated

---

[96]   GCF. 2019. *Lao PDR Country Programme*. Vientiane.

[97]   World Bank Climate Change Knowledge Portal. *Laos: Climate Data Projections* (accessed 7 February 2020).

[98]   World Bank. 2008. *Lao PDR: Policy Markets and Agricultural transition in Northern Uplands*. Washington, DC, cited in Government of Lao PDR, LWU. 2018. *Lao PDR Gender Profile*. Vientiane.

[99]   Government of Lao PDR, Statistics Bureau. 2011. *Lao Census of Agriculture, 2010–2011*. Vientiane.

[100] ADB. *Key Indicator Data Base Lao PDR* (accessed 2 June 2021); World Food Programme (WFP). 2017. Executive Board First Regular Session (20–23 February 2017). Rome, cited in WFP. 2017. *Lao PDR Country Strategic Plan (2017–2021)*. Rome. para. 11.

[101] Food and Agriculture Organization of the United Nations (FAO). 2018. *Country Gender Assessment of Agriculture and the Rural Sector in Lao People's Democratic Republic*. Vientiane.

[102] Government of Lao PDR, MoNRE, and WFP. 2016. *Lao PDR: CLEAR – Consolidated Livelihood Exercise for Analyzing Resilience*. Vientiane.

rice is the dominant seasonal crop, followed by upland rice and cereals.[103] Livelihoods that are dependent on highland rice paddies are the most at risk of climate change impacts, as the rugged terrain in these remote areas limits access to land and opportunities for livelihood diversification and, in turn, their ability to develop resilience.[104]

Agriculture in the Lao PDR is in transition from subsistence to commercial production, which has benefited rural communities by stimulating economic growth and poverty reduction.[105] The commercialization of agriculture has created opportunities for households to boost their income by growing cash crops, which has driven the unsustainable use of natural resources and environmental degradation, partly assisted by the limited enforcement of local crop management regulations.[106] This has been linked to extensive land degradation.[107] The transition has also disadvantaged women in non-Lao Tai ethnic groups, who may have limited Lao language skills and lack experience conducting business in a cash economy.[108] The Lao PDR does not have social safety nets in place for those whose livelihoods suffer as a result of the transition to commercial agriculture (footnote 118).

The Government of the Lao People's Democratic Republic often classifies forestry as part of the agriculture sector. The government set the target of 70% forest cover by 2020 and placed a logging ban on much forestland to harness forests as a carbon sink and mitigate the effects of flooding.[109] However, the proportion of forested land area has fallen short of this goal—being closer to 60%—partly due to illegal logging and inadequate legal enforcement mechanisms.[110] The government aims to open up the scope for increased forestry activity while striking a balance with forest conservation goals.[111] For example, in January 2021, The Lao PDR signed an agreement with the World Bank Forest Carbon Partnership Facility to reduce deforestation and promote sustainable rural land use in six provinces.[112]

Both agriculture and forestry in the Lao PDR are vulnerable to climate change-related natural hazards. Agriculture—including fisheries and forestry—was the most adversely impacted sector in the devastating 2018 floods, suffering 57% of the Lao PDR total economic losses.[113] Variations in the natural hydrological cycle—due to floods, droughts, and storms in the context of climate change—are likely to pose severe threats to agricultural production, particularly to rain-fed crop production.[114] The intensive use of groundwater due to drought is expected to reduce overall rice production by up to 10% by 2050, with significant consequences for food security and economic development.[115] Building resilience to disasters is a critical issue for the sector, with key measures including moving away from monocultures, diversifying livelihoods, improving farmers' access to financial capital, and improving infrastructure.[116] Due to the gendered division of labor and direct and indirect discrimination, women and men may not have equal access to these measures. With this context, it is necessary to understand how women and men experience and respond to changes in the agriculture sector.

103   FAO. 2018. *Country Gender Assessment of Agriculture and the Rural Sector in Lao People's Democratic Republic.* Vientiane.
104   Government of Lao PDR, MoNRE, and WFP. 2016. *Lao PDR: CLEAR – Consolidated Livelihood Exercise for Analyzing Resilience.* Vientiane.
105   Government of Lao PDR, LWU. 2018. *Lao PDR Gender Profile.* Vientiane.
106   UNDRR. 2019. *Disaster Risk Reduction in Lao PDR: Status Report 2019.* Bangkok. pp. 12; CARE. 2016. *Elevating Farmers' Resilience: Baseline Assessment of the Project "Northern Upland Promoting Climate Resilience."* Vientiane.
107   UNDRR. 2019. Disaster Risk Reduction in Lao PDR: Status Report 2019. Bangkok.
108   World Bank. 2008. *Lao PDR: Policy Markets and Agricultural transition in Northern Uplands.* Washington, DC, cited in Government of Lao PDR, LWU. 2018. *Lao PDR Gender Profile.* Vientiane.
109   UNDRR. 2019. *Disaster Risk Reduction in Lao PDR: Status Report 2019.* Bangkok.
110   United Nations. 2019. *2018 Progress Report: Lao PDR-United Nations Partnership Framework 2017–2021.* Vientiane; UNDRR. 2019. *Disaster Risk Reduction in Lao PDR: Status Report 2019.* Bangkok.
111   United Nations. 2019. *2018 Progress Report: Lao PDR-United Nations Partnership Framework 2017–2021.* Vientiane.
112   World Bank. 2021. *Lao PDR Signs Agreement to Protect Forests and Reduce Carbon Emissions.* 27 January.
113   Government of Lao PDR. 2018. *Post-Disaster Needs Assessment (PDNA) 2018 Floods Lao PDR.* Vientiane.
114   Government of Lao PDR, MoNRE, and WFP. 2016. *Lao PDR: CLEAR – Consolidated Livelihood Exercise for Analyzing Resilience.* Vientiane; UNDRR. 2019. *Disaster Risk Reduction in Lao PDR: Status Report 2019.* Bangkok.
115   UNDRR. 2019. *Disaster Risk Reduction in Lao PDR: Status Report 2019.* Bangkok.
116   Government of Lao PDR. 2018. *Post-Disaster Needs Assessment (PDNA) 2018 Floods Lao PDR.* Vientiane; Government of Lao PDR, MoNRE, and WFP. 2016. *Lao PDR: CLEAR – Consolidated Livelihood Exercise for Analyzing Resilience.* Vientiane.

2.4.2 Gender Issues in the Agriculture Sector

Women comprise over half of the agricultural workforce and contribute significantly to all parts of agricultural production in the Lao PDR. However, a gender division of labor commonly exists where women's contribution is often undervalued as it includes unpaid household and off-farm labor.[117] The burden on women in agriculture is increasing further as many men migrate to urban areas for work (footnote 127). A greater percentage of female-headed farming households grow low land or irrigated rice than male-headed farming households and, generally, female-headed households have a less diversified crop, rendering them less resilient to the adverse effects of climate change and disasters.[118] Similarly, men and women have different roles in forestry (Box 2). Men often control the most valuable forest resources, leaving women restricted to products yielding a more limited income.[119]

A critical gender issue in the agriculture sector of the Lao PDR is women's access to land. Land titles enable women to access loans using their land as collateral to invest in agricultural tools, technologies, and climate-smart agricultural practices.[120] The challenges women face in attaining documentation for landownership contribute to women's lower levels of access to financial services relative to men.[121] Land rights improve women's adaptive capacity to the impacts of climate change as secure land tenure provides greater certainty of access to land in the event of a disaster and underpins the ability of people to return to their livelihoods, food production, and rebuilding activities.[122] Although the Lao PDR has operated a land titling system since the mid-1990s, only about one-third of registered land parcels have been titled. The ongoing land titling process is an opportunity to ensure that women have equal access to land, although it would need to include specific measures to address customary practices that prohibit women's inheritance of land (footnote 132).

Another key gender equality issue in the agriculture sector is that women participate in local natural resource management at even lower rates than in regional and national governance (section 1.5). This is because the Law on Local Administration (Article 91) provides that village meetings must be attended by household heads, who are traditionally men.[123] The 2015 census reported that 87% of all households are headed by men,[124] but this figure is 91% among farming households and 92.6% for rural households in villages without roads.[125] Also, land title is often a prerequisite for participation in community decision making and resource management, limiting women's opportunities to participate and lead.[126] Consequently, women are significantly underrepresented in a sector in which they comprise an increasing majority of laborers.

An emerging gender issue in the agriculture sector is the health impacts of agricultural chemicals. The 2011 Lao Census of Agriculture found that female-headed farming households were slightly more likely to use chemical fertilizers and pesticides than male-headed farming households, possibly because they are used to save labor.[127] Women and children are particularly exposed to the health impacts of these chemicals, as women are

---

[117]   Government of Lao PDR, LWU. 2018. *Lao PDR Gender Profile*. Vientiane.

[118]   UNDRR. 2019. *Disaster Risk Reduction in Lao PDR: Status Report 2019*. Bangkok; Government of Lao PDR. 2018. *Post-Disaster Needs Assessment (PDNA) 2018 Floods Lao PDR*. Vientiane; Government of Lao PDR, MoNRE, and WFP. 2016. *Lao PDR: CLEAR – Consolidated Livelihood Exercise for Analyzing Resilience*. Vientiane.

[119]   Climate Investment Funds (CIF). 2017. *Gender and Sustainable Forest Management: Entry Points for Design and Implementation*. Washington, DC.

[120]   D. Fletschner, and L. Kenney. 2014. *Rural Women's Access to Financial Services: Credit, Savings, and Insurance*. Gender in Agriculture: Closing the Knowledge Gap. 11. pp. 187–208; P. Antwi-Agyei et al. 2015. Impacts of Land Tenure Arrangements on The Adaptive Capacity of Marginalised Groups: The Case of Ghana's Ejura Sekyedumase And Bongo Districts. *Land Use Policy*. 49. pp. 203–212.

[121]   FAO. 2018. *Country Gender Assessment of Agriculture and the Rural Sector in Lao People's Democratic Republic*. Vientiane.

[122]   CIF. 2017. *Gender and Sustainable Forest Management: Entry Points for Design and Implementation*. Washington, DC; UN Women. 2016. Leveraging Co-Benefits Between Gender Equality and Climate Action for Sustainable Development. New York.

[123]   FAO. 2018. *Country Gender Assessment of Agriculture and the Rural Sector in Lao People's Democratic Republic*. Vientiane.

[124]   Government of Lao PDR, Statistics Bureau. 2017. Statistical Yearbook 2016. Vientiane.

[125]   FAO. 2018. *Country Gender Assessment of Agriculture and the Rural Sector in Lao People's Democratic Republic*. Vientiane.

[126]   CIF. 2017. *Gender and Sustainable Forest Management: Entry Points for Design and Implementation*. Washington, DC; Global Gender and Climate Alliance. 2016. *Gender and Climate Change: A Closer Look at Existing Evidence*. New York.

[127]   Government of Lao PDR, MAF, and FAO. 2011. *Lao Census of Agriculture, 2010–2011*; FAO. 2018. *Country Gender Assessment of Agriculture and the Rural Sector in Lao People's Democratic Republic*. Vientiane.

typically responsible for spreading them among crops, often while carrying children.[128] The Food and Agriculture Organization of the United Nations (FAO) has called for further research on this as an "emerging concern for rural women and children's health" (footnote 138, p. 32).

2.4.3 Overview of Laws and Policies Related to the Agriculture Sector

The central legislative instrument for agriculture is the Law on Land 2019, which supersedes a 1997 version of the law and provides that all land in the Lao PDR is owned by the national community.[129] The state acts as the holder of ownership and grants long-term and secure land use rights to persons, collectives, and organizations (Article 3). Land is allocated according to the Land Allocation Master Plan (Part II) and has classifications, including "agricultural land" and "forestland" (Article 20). Land use purposes are divided into two categories: conservation purposes and development purposes (being agricultural production for food security and related matters) (Article 19). The management and use of agricultural land must comply with the Land Allocation Master Plan, which focuses on productivity increase and movement towards intensive agricultural practices (Article 37). Part VI (Articles 92 to 105) sets out new processes for land registration, including the establishment of a "one door service," wherein district officers from Ministry of Natural Resources and Environment can conduct land title registration (Articles 28 and 101).

Another important law is the Law on Resettlement and Vocation 2018, which regulates the planned resettlement and reallocation of vocations by the government.[130] Its purpose is to provide resettlement and vocation when people are displaced or migrate within the Lao PDR, and to solve problems that occur due to unregulated relocations, to reduce poverty, and improve livelihoods (Articles 1 and 2). There are two categories of resettlement: specific resettlement for people affected by development projects, and general resettlement for people in remote and undeveloped areas including "high risk living areas" (Article 11). "High risk living areas" are areas where frequent or intense natural hazards occur, although the law does not address emergency displacements (Article 14). Provisions relating to "high risk living areas" (Article 14) are most relevant to women's climate change and disaster resilience.

Two other important legislative instruments on agriculture include the Law on Agriculture 1998,[131] and the Law on Forestry 2007, which is under revision as of 2021 and as such is not considered for gender analysis in this report.[132] The Lao PDR also has several key policies for the agriculture sector, of which three are due for revision as of 2021 and are not gender analyzed in this report: the Forestry Strategy 2020,[133] the Poverty-Focused Agricultural Development Plan (2003–2020),[134] and the Strategy for Agricultural Development (2011–2020).[135] Another key policy is the Lao PDR National Agro-Biodiversity Program and Action Plan (2015–2025), which establishes goals for preserving the biodiversity of organisms used for food and agriculture to be implemented by a range of ministries, departments, and development partners such as UNDP.[136]

The key government institution relating to agriculture is the Ministry of Agriculture and Forestry (MAF), which oversees the implementation of policies on natural resource management, forestry, food security, and agriculture.[137] Under MAF, the Department of Agricultural Land Management is designing the Land Resources Information

[128]   FAO. 2018. *Country Gender Assessment of Agriculture and the Rural Sector in Lao People's Democratic Republic*. Vientiane.
[129]   Government of Lao PDR. 2003. *Land Law*. Vientiane.
[130]   Government of Lao PDR. 2018. *Law on Resettlement and Vocation*. Vientiane.
[131]   Government of Lao PDR. 1998. *Law on Agriculture 1998*. Vientiane.
[132]   Government of Lao PDR. 2007. *Forestry Law 2007*. Vientiane.
[133]   Government of Lao PDR. 2005. *Forestry Strategy to the Year 2020 of the Lao PDR* . Vientiane.
[134]   Government of Lao PDR. 2003. *Poverty-Focused Agricultural Development Plan (2003–2020) in National Growth and Poverty Eradication Strategy (NGPES)*. Vientiane.
[135]   Government of Lao PDR. 2011. *Strategy for Agricultural Development (2011–2020)*. Vientiane.
[136]   Government of Lao PDR. 2016. *Lao PDR National Agro-Biodiversity Programme and Action Plan II (2015–2025)*. Vientiane.
[137]   Government of Lao PDR, Land Portal. N.d. *Lao Ministry of Agriculture and Forestry*.

Management System, intended to model climate change scenarios for long-term government planning on land distribution and use.[138]

2.4.4 Gender Analysis Summary of Agriculture Laws and Policies

A gender analysis was conducted of laws and policies relevant to agriculture (Table 5). The color coded system is used to categorize the laws and policies and demonstrates the state of gender mainstreaming as of 2021.

Table 5: Summary of Gender Inclusion in Agriculture Laws and Policies

Law/Policy	Summary of Gender References
Law on Land 2019	It does not differentiate between the needs and interests of women and men, instead referring only to "citizens" or "individuals." It does not include the principles of equality and nondiscrimination.
Law on Resettlement and Vocation 2018	The law uses gender-neutral language. It does not recognize how gender may impact the experiences of different people in resettlement and vocation or mention equality.
Law on Forestry 2007	It does not refer to gender and instead refers to "households" and "individuals." It does not consider gender or social issues or include the principles of equality and nondiscrimination.
Law on Agriculture 1998	It does not refer to women and instead refers to "farmers." The law does not reference or consider gender or social issues or mention equality.
National Agro-Biodiversity Program and Action Plan 2021–2025	It notes that men and women have different roles in and understandings of the management and use of agro-biodiversity resources, which "need to be fully incorporated in all biodiversity management plans" (2.1, p. 6). It does not mention the principles of equality and nondiscrimination.

Note: Color coding: gender responsive (green), gender sensitive (yellow), not yet gender mainstreamed (orange).
Source: Asian Development Bank.

The Law on Resettlement and Vocation 2018 is not yet gender mainstreamed and disadvantages women in important ways. Under the law, an affected person needs to have legal documents evidencing land use rights—including customary land use—for specific resettlement due to a development project (Articles 20, 22[1] and 21[4]). Without such documents, an affected person is unable to receive any compensation or damages, except for buildings, trees, and produce. Women are less likely to have their names on land titles and so are adversely affected by this provision. Additionally, the law provides few consultation opportunities; only limited rights to participate in consultations for people being resettled (Article 46[4]) or receiving a new vocation (Article 48[6]). The topics of these consultations are limited to already developed resettlement/compensation plans or vocational/livelihood plans. The law does not require consultation at earlier points in time—such as during studies or strategy development (Articles 9 and 10)—and there is no legal requirement for the studies undertaken by the project owner to consider the interests and concerns of women as distinct from those of men. Given that women are underrepresented in governance at all levels in the Lao PDR (section 1.5), without consultation their input into resettlement and vocation reallocations is limited. Consequently, women's concerns relating to the agriculture sector may be overlooked, reducing their ability to build resilience to the impacts of climate change and disasters.

The National Agro-Biodiversity Program and Action Plan 2021–2025 goes some way toward gender sensitivity, as it acknowledges the different roles that men and women play in managing and using agro-biodiversity resources and calls for the incorporation of their knowledge into management plans.[139] However, it does not provide detailed guidance on incorporating gender into the implementation of the program or address the inequalities inherent in the gendered division of labor in agriculture and forestry in the Lao PDR, such as women's lower rates of landownership.

---

[138]   United Nations. 2019. *2018 Progress Report: Lao PDR-United Nations Partnership Framework 2017–2021*. Vientiane; Government of Lao PDR. 2018. *Post-Disaster Needs Assessment (PDNA) 2018 Floods Lao PDR*. Vientiane.

[139]   Government of Lao PDR. 2016. *Lao PDR National Agro-Biodiversity Programme and Action Plan II (2015–2025)*. Vientiane.

The action plan is not gender mainstreamed, except for the requirement for gender-disaggregated farmer surveys on agro-biodiversity conservation (Outcome 3). This could be built upon to require the collection of qualitative and quantitative sex-disaggregated data on agriculture and forestry. The gathering of disaggregated data on the agriculture sector would be beneficial for designing gender responsive laws and policies that support women's resilience to climate change and disasters. This data should include quantitative and qualitative sex-disaggregated data on past flood impacts, as well as similar data from areas identified as high risk for climate change and disasters in the future, including undertaking pilot studies to improve women's involvement in decision making in village committees.

Overall, laws and policies in the Lao PDR relating to agriculture lack reference to the essential concepts of equality and nondiscrimination, despite the significant barriers women face in accessing land and finance and participating in decision making in this area. By taking a gender-neutral approach, these laws and policies miss opportunities to promote women's full and equal participation in agriculture and generate substantive equality. For example, the Law on Land 2019 does not specifically allow for—or encourage—matrimonial land acquired during marriage to be registered under the names of both husband and wife (Articles 100–102), which is a step backward from the 2003 Land Law, which made these provisions in Article 43.[140] None of the laws or policies require gender analysis or gender mainstreaming and only the National Agro-Biodiversity Program and Action Plan requires the collection of sex-disaggregated data. There are also no references to the LGE, which would support the provision and use of such tools to address gender inequalities in agriculture law and policies. Given the importance of agriculture to rural livelihoods in the Lao PDR, promoting women's equal access to land and participation in decision making would strengthen women's resilience to the impacts of climate change and disasters.

2.5 Strengthening the Socioeconomic Resilience of Women

Strengthening women's resilience requires more than developing and applying gender sensitive and responsive laws and policies that are specifically directed to climate change and disasters. As presented, these phenomena occur within existing social and economic structures in which there are already different gender roles, as well as gender discrimination and inequalities that influence how disasters and climate change affect women and men.

This subsection focuses on a selection of national laws that build women's socioeconomic resilience as outlined in the National Good Practice Legislative Framework for Strengthening Women's Resilience to Climate Change and Disasters (Figure 1). It includes laws preventing violence against women and girls, laws on land, inheritance, access to finance, education and training, and decent employment (formal and informal), among others. Given the enormous scope, the following three major themes were selected for their greatest immediate relevance to women's resilience to climate and disaster risk:

(i)   combating violence against women and girls;
(ii) improving women's rights to assets; and
(iii) improving women's access to decent work.

These are all identified in the Ulaanbaatar Declaration, adopted by the International Conference on Sustainable Development Goals: Gender and Development, as well as in CEDAW GR37.[141] The following subsections are presented as a discussion, not as summary tables similar to the previous sections because there is often only one law or policy covering each area, or in some cases several laws some of which have already been discussed.

---

[140]   Government of Lao PDR. 2003. *Land Law*. Vientiane.
[141]   Asian Ministerial Conference on Disaster Risk Reduction. 2018. *Ulaanbaatar Declaration*. Ulaanbaatar. para. 12.

2.5.1 Combating Violence Against Women and Girls

Violence against women (VAW) is a form of gender discrimination that reduces women's health and well-being, impacts their livelihoods through lost time in work or education, and increases their vulnerability to shocks. Overall, it inhibits women's social and economic capacity to reduce their risk, respond to and recover from disasters, adapt to climate change, and participate in emerging opportunities such as in the green economy. As of 2021, there is no reference to GBV or VAW in the context of disaster or climate change laws or policies in the Lao PDR.

The Lao PDR has two key laws highly relevant to GBV: the Law on Preventing and Combatting Violence against Women and Children 2014[142] and the Law on Development and Protection of Women 2004.[143] The Law on Preventing and Combatting Violence against Women and Children 2014 is a comprehensive law that defines violence against women and children (Articles 2 and 10–17) and outlines measures to combat it (Articles 31, 47, 51, and 79). The Law on Development and Protection of Women 2004 defines and outlines mediation measures to address "domestic violence" against women and children (Articles 29–32, and 35–36). Both laws refer to the need to change discriminatory cultural beliefs, but promote settlement and mediation of VAW, even for criminal offenses. In the case of violence that "does not cause much harm," either mediation or judicial proceedings can be applied, but "if the violence is serious" it must be settled by judicial proceedings (Article 47). These categories are highly subjective, and the distinction socially legitimizes VAW.[144] The laws also do not clearly define "minor offenses," guide the circumstances in which mediation processes may be lawfully undertaken, or mandate the training of mediators. Therefore, they do not follow CEDAW General Recommendations Nos. 33 and 35, which provide that states should ensure that cases of VAW are not referred to alternative dispute resolution procedures, and especially not as a mandatory requirement.[145] These laws contain elements that reinforce gender discrimination and can impede women's access to formal justice for VAW in courts.

The National Plan of Action on Protection and Elimination of Violence Against Women and Children (2021–2025)—a policy in draft form as of 2021—is also relevant, as it aims to develop a coherent multisector approach to preventing and addressing GBV. The Commission for Advancement of Women and Mothers and Children will be responsible for monitoring and evaluating the plan's implementation, including collecting data on the experiences of victims and/or survivors of GBV. This is a promising step forward, although such data should be disaggregated and collected ethically and sensitively, as outlined in United Nations Population Fund (UNFPA) Minimum Initial Standards Package Standard 4.[146] In finalizing the National Plan of Action, the government can be guided by the recommendations made by the CEDAW Committee in its 2018 concluding observations in paragraphs 24 and 26.[147] This includes developing and implementing the plan in a participatory and inclusive process. Also, to provide capacity-building programs for judges, prosecutors, the police and other law enforcement officials, and members of village mediation units to ensure that all cases of gender-based violence are investigated and prosecuted in a gender-sensitive manner.

These areas of particular concern are relevant to the discussion on strengthening women's resilience as rural women and girls often face significant disadvantage due to the absence of social protection schemes including access to essential services (which provide shelter and service centers are considered to be) both during and following disasters. Globally, women experiencing intersecting forms of discrimination—such as ethnic minority women or women with disabilities—lack physical access to services, and barriers to communication during and

---

[142]   Government of Lao PDR. 2014. *Law on Preventing and Combatting Violence against Women and Children.* Vientiane.

[143]   Government of Lao PDR. 2004. *Law on Development and Protection of Women.* Vientiane.

[144]   CEDAW. 2009. *Concluding Observations of the Committee on the Elimination of Discrimination Against Women: Lao People's Democratic Republic.* CEDAW/C/LAO/CO/7. 14 August. para 23.

[145]   CEDAW. 2015. *General Recommendation No. 33 on Women's Access to Justice.* CEDAW/C/GC/33. 23 July. para. 58(c); CEDAW. 2017. *General Recommendation No. 35 on Gender-Based Violence Against Women, Updating General Recommendation No. 19.* CEDAW/C/GC/35. 14 July. para 45.

[146]   UNFPA. 2015. *Minimum Standards for Prevention and Response to Gender Based Violence in Emergencies.* New York.

[147]   CEDAW. 2018. *Concluding observations on the combined eighth and ninth periodic reports of the Lao People's Democratic Republic CEDAW/C/LAO/CO/8-9.* 14 November. paras. 24 and 26.

after disasters heighten their risk of violence.[148] The prevalence and nature of domestic violence in the Lao PDR points to the need to address this issue urgently. As part of this effort, data and evidence on the prevalence of VAW in the context of disasters and climate change need to be gathered.

2.5.2 Improving Women's Rights to Assets

CEDAW GR37 notes that women—specifically rural and indigenous women involved in food and agriculture work—are directly affected by disasters and climate change (footnote 158). CEDAW GR37 acknowledges that women make up the majority of global small and subsistence farmers, and a significant proportion is farmworkers. Consequently—due to discriminatory laws and social norms—women often have limited access to secure land tenure. As discussed in section 2.4, legal and socially recognized landownership can be necessary for effective adaptation to changing climatic conditions. Access to land and inheritance rights are crucial for women's resilience to climate change and disasters.

Since the mid-1990s, the Government of the Lao People's Democratic Republic has been implementing a land titling program (LTP1 and LTP2), which has increased women's inclusion on land titles. However, issues remain in rural areas, in which most rural land users—including women—do not have legal documentation to ensure the security of tenure (section 2.4).[149] Under the Constitution, men and women have equal status concerning property and inheritance rights, including land rights (Article 17),[150] although traditional succession practices often affect women's inheritance of land.[151] Therefore, a combination of legislation, advocacy, and enforcement is required to change traditional practices and beliefs that indirectly or directly discriminate against women.[152]

Land security for women needs to improve in advance of further climate change and disasters. The key to this is ensuring that there is sufficient and relevant sex-disaggregated land information and data to enable targeted approaches to promote women's land rights. This needs to include not only quantitative but qualitative information, as the registration of women on land may also be connected to stereotypes around women's roles in agriculture and forestry.

Inheritance rights and housing are other key areas that are vital for women as they are connected to poverty and inextricably linked with economic autonomy. These rights are highly important to strengthening women's economic resilience to disasters and climate change. The relevant law on inheritance and property in the Lao PDR—the Law on Inheritance 2008—expresses equality between women, men, boys, and girls. It provides for equal distribution among all children except for stepchildren, with no difference between the rights of males and females (Article 15), and provides for the inheritance rights of unborn children (Article 16).[153] However, in practice, succession tends to follow customary practices, which vary among ethnic groups.[154]

Customary practices often prevail over the law regarding land and property inheritance, although sex-disaggregated national data on land and property ownership is limited. A 2018 survey of 224,000 land titles by MoNRE found that 31.3% were registered under a woman's name, 22.3% in the name of a man, 38.9% in the name of both a man and woman, and 6.3% under the name of others.[155] However, as the data were mainly collected in areas where the matrilineal and matrilocal social systems are dominant—and where many women inherit land from their parents—

[148] CEDAW. 2018. *General Recommendation No. 37 On the Gender-Related Dimensions of Disaster Risk Reduction in The Context of Climate Change.* CEDAW/C/GC/37. 7 February.
[149] FAO. 2018. *Country Gender Assessment of Agriculture and the Rural Sector in Lao People's Democratic Republic.* Vientiane.
[150] Government of Lao PDR. 1991. *Constitution of the Lao People's Democratic Republic 1991 (Rev. 2003).* Vientiane.
[151] LWU. 2018. *Lao PDR Gender Profile.* Vientiane.
[152] International Development Law Organization. 2010. *Women's Inheritance and Property Rights: A Vehicle to Accelerate Progress Towards the Achievement of the Millennium Development Goals.* Rome.
[153] Government of Lao PDR. 2008. *Law on Inheritance.* Vientiane.
[154] LWU. 2018. *Lao PDR Gender Profile.* Vientiane. pp. 55; FAO. N.d. Gender and Land Rights Database: Laos (accessed 1 July 2021).
[155] Land Information Working Group. 2020. *Women and Land Rights in Lao PDR: Rural Transformation and a Dream of Secure Tenure.* Vientiane.

the national figures for women's landownership are likely to be significantly lower (footnote 165). The Government of the Lao People's Democratic Republic does not collect sex-disaggregated data on SDG gender indicators on land rights.[156] A recent study of seven villages in Vientiane, Savannakhet, Oudomxay, and Phongsali provinces, found that women had lost access and control over land in all seven villages surveyed due to rural transformations and/or patrilineal inheritance practices that give sons preference over daughters.[157] There is also some evidence of erosion of women's traditional rights to land in various areas due to the commercialization of agriculture and/or infrastructure development in the Lao PDR (footnote 167).[158] There is limited public information available on women's rates of homeownership. The 4th Population and Housing Census 2015 found that 13.2% of households were headed by women and that 96% of households owned the dwelling unit they occupied, although it did not capture whether homes were owned by the head of household or disaggregate ownership by sex.[159] It is time for research to be undertaken to determine the extent to which women can inherit land on an equal basis as men in practice, particularly in rural areas.

Inheritance law and practice is a source of serious discrimination against women, who often inherit a smaller share of property from their husband or father compared with widowers and sons.[160] In some instances, women are granted limited and controlled rights, such as receiving income only from the property of the deceased. Inequalities in inheritance rights and housing in the Lao PDR pose a compounding concern in the pursuit of strengthening women's resilience.

2.5.3 General Improvement of Decent Work for Women

The final socioeconomic area covered in this report is that of decent work. As defined by the International Labour Organization (ILO), decent work encompasses "opportunities for work that is productive and delivers a fair income, security in the workplace and social protection for families, better prospects for personal development and social integration, freedom for people to express their concerns, organize and participate in the decisions that affect their lives and equality of opportunity and treatment for all women and men."[161] The key issues selected for this report that affect decent work for women in the Lao PDR are sexual harassment and discrimination in employment, lower remuneration compared to men doing work of the same value, access to a minimum wage, and financial capital. These issues impact the ability of women to gain and remain in decent work, and to build the economic security to manage shocks caused by climate change and disasters.

Workplace sexual harassment is a form of human rights violation[162] and GBV.[163] As noted in the country profile, the Lao PDR has a high incidence and prevalence of GBV—including sexual harassment—but very low reporting rates, as women often fear the social stigma that may result.[164] Consequently, the Lao PDR has limited official data and information on workplace sexual harassment and a lack of research on the issue.[165] The key law on workplace sexual harassment is the Law on Labor 2014, which prohibits employers from violating the personal rights of employees—especially female employees—through speech, sight, text, touch, or touching inappropriate

---

[156]   UN Women. N.d. *Lao People's Democratic Republic* (accessed 1 July 2021); Government of Lao PDR. 2018. *Lao People's Democratic Republic: Voluntary National Review on the Implementation of the 2030 Agenda for Sustainable Development.* Vientiane.

[157]   Land Information Working Group. 2020. *Women and Land Rights in Lao PDR: Rural Transformation and a Dream of Secure Tenure.* Vientiane.

[158]   LWU. 2018. *Lao PDR Gender Profile.* Vientiane.

[159]   Government of Lao PDR, Statistics Bureau. 2015. *Results of Population and Housing Census 2015.* Vientiane.

[160]   The Global Initiative for Economic, Social and Cultural Rights. n.d. *Using CEDAW to Secure Women's Land and Property Rights: A Practical Guide.* Duluth, MN, USA.

[161]   ILO. N.d. *Decent Work.*

[162]   CEDAW. 1989. *CEDAW General Recommendation No. 12: Violence Against Women.*

[163]   CEDAW. 1992. *General Recommendation No. 19: Violence Against Women.*

[164]   Government of Lao PDR, National Commission for the Advancement of Women. 2016. *Lao National Survey on Women's Health and Life Experiences 2014.* Vientiane.

[165]   Association for Development of Women and Legal Education. 2017. *Sexual Harassment in Workplace in Vientiane Capital.* Vientiane.

areas (Section 141[4]).[166] The law allows a worker to end an employment contract in the event of harassment or sexual harassment, either perpetrated by the employer or if the employer ignores sexual harassment (Section 83[4]), footnote 176). However, these provisions do not protect workers from all forms of sexual harassment or provide for adequate remedies or sanctions. As observed by the ILO Committee of Experts on the Application of Conventions and Recommendations, the law also does not provide a clear definition of "harassment" or "sexual harassment in the workplace."[167] This ambiguity limits the extent to which the rights of employees that experience sexual harassment—who are disproportionately women—are protected.

The second issue is that in the Lao PDR, women continue to receive lower wages than men in many sectors of the economy.[168] In 2017, the country had a gender wage gap of 15.3% (footnote 178). The ILO Equal Remuneration Convention (C100)—which the Lao PDR has ratified—does not refer only to "equal work" (being the same work) or to "equal working conditions" (being the same working conditions). Instead, the ILO requirement is to ensure equal remuneration for work or working conditions that may be quite different, but of "equal value." Work of "equal value" may be as different as heavy lifting in factory work (often done by men), to dexterity in inserting parts into machines in a factory (often done by women). This is an important distinction and is frequently the cause of gender wage gaps. However, the Law on Labor 2014 no longer refers to "work of equal value" as in its previous iteration, and instead provides that "female employees shall receive a salary or wages equal to that of male employees, excepting some forms of work that has negative effects upon the reproductive health of women, which must be protected in every case" (Article 96). This does not conform with the ILO C100. Likewise, the provisions of the LGE[169] (Articles 10 and 14) and the Law on the Development and Protection of Women 2004 (Section 15), do not comply with the convention. [170]

Another compounding issue facing women's access to decent work in the Lao PDR is that not all women have access to a minimum wage, although there have been significant improvements. There is significant international evidence that minimum wages reduce overall inequality by raising pay at the bottom of the distribution relative to the middle.[171] There is also evidence that setting national minimum wages reduces inequality of wages and remuneration between women and men.[172] As women tend to be at the bottom end of income distribution, a minimum wage sets a wage floor that improves wage levels for women.[173] Under the Law on Labor 2014, the Government of the Lao People's Democratic Republic sets minimum wages based on consultations with third parties and is not required to consider minimum wage setting concerning gender.[174] The ILO and the government established a Decent Work Country Program (2017–2021), which supports a new tripartite committee to develop criteria and procedures for minimum wage setting and conduct regular gender-sensitive reviews of minimum wages, with a specific target for implementation in 2021. [175] It also set the country's first minimum wages for unskilled labor in 2018, and for the garment and footwear industries—which are primarily comprised of female workers— in 2019 (footnote 185). There is still room for improvement as some sectors in which many women work—such as agriculture—do not have a minimum wage. Overall, the Lao PDR's Decent Work Country Program has made significant progress towards the provision of a minimum wage across all sectors, which will support women's access to decent work.

166   Government of Lao PDR. 2014. *Law on Labor (Amended)*. [Unofficial Translation]. Vientiane.
167   ILO. 2020. Observation (CEACR) - Adopted 2020, Published 109th ILC Session (2021).
168   P. Siliphong and K. Phoumphon. 2019. *Gender, Employment and Wage Disparities in Laos*. Phnom Penh: CDRI.
169   Government of Lao PDR. 2019. *Law on Gender Equality*. [Unofficial Translation]. Vientiane.
170   Government of Lao PDR. 2004. *Law on Development and Protection of Women*. Vientiane.
171   J. Healy. 2009. *The Wages Safety Net of the Australian Industrial Relations Commission, 1993–2005*. Adelaide, Australia.
172   ADB. 2013. *Good Global Legal Practices to Promote Gender Equality in the Labor Market*. Manila.
173   J. Romeyn et al. 2011. *Review of Equal Remuneration Principles*. Canberra, Australia.
174   Government of Lao PDR. 2014. *Law on Labor 2014 (Amended)*. [Unofficial Translation]. Vientiane.
175   ILO and Government of Lao PDR. *Decent Work Country Program (DWCP) for Lao PDR 2017–2021*. Vientiane.

Finally, women face challenges to access capital and support for business development in the Lao PDR. In 2015, more than 40% of all enterprises in the Lao PDR were at least partially owned by women, and most newly registered enterprises in urban areas were owned by women.[176] This is a potential increasing source of decent work and economic autonomy for women in the Lao PDR. Enterprises owned by women in the Lao PDR are typically smaller and employ fewer workers than those owned by men.[177] In 2014, the Lao Businesswomen's Association characterized the majority of women-run businesses as micro in scale and attributed the limited growth of women-owned enterprises to a lack of systems in place to support them.[178] They also face challenges in accessing capital, as financial services from the commercial banking system are out of reach for most women-owned enterprises, especially those in rural areas. Instead, many use savings and credit services through formal and informal microfinance opportunities (footnote 188). The only relevant law in the Lao PDR is the Law on the Promotion of Small and Medium Sized Enterprises 2011, which includes a provision on creating entrepreneurs, "especially female entrepreneurs" (Article 17), but provides no further references to gender or guidance on gender sensitive implementation.[179]

Decent work includes important ingredients for strengthening the economic resilience of women to climate change and disasters: improving the types of jobs that women perform and their remuneration for those jobs; upholding women's rights to live and work free from harassment; and ensuring their access to financial resources—and by extension—their economic autonomy. The LGE significantly bolsters the rights of women across these areas and can be used to gender mainstream across laws and policies to strengthen women's resilience to climate change and disaster risk.

[176]   United States Agency for International Development (USAid). 2016. *The Ecosystem for Women's Entrepreneurship in Lao PDR*. Washington, DC.
[177]   Keovialey, R. 2018. *Overview of Women's Entrepreneurship in Micro, Small and Medium Enterprises in Lao PDR*.
[178]   USAid. 2016. *The Ecosystem for Women's Entrepreneurship in Lao PDR*. Washington, DC.
[179]   Government of Lao PDR. 2011. *Law on the Promotion of Small and Medium Sized Enterprises 2011*. Vientiane.

3 Conclusion and Recommendations

The purpose of this report was to conduct a gender analysis of the national legal and policy frameworks of the Lao PDR to determine the extent to which laws, policies, and strategies consider gender inequalities in climate and disaster risk and contribute to strengthening women's resilience. The analysis found that the LGE is gender responsive, as it mandates gender mainstreaming in all areas of work, although it does not provide for substantive equality or prohibit both direct and indirect discrimination as fitting with international standards in the (CEDAW Convention). The plan for its implementation—the NAPGE—is gender responsive, ambitious, and includes a broad spectrum of gender positive targets. However, there is limited adoption and translation of the LGE in key sector laws and policies, and NAPGE is still in the early stages of implementation. Laws and policies that affect women's resilience to climate change and disasters in the Lao PDR are not yet gender mainstreamed, except for the EIA Decree. The EIA Decree is classified as gender sensitive due to its requirement for the collection of information and conducting of assessments relating to gender, which will produce a baseline of sex-disaggregated data and essentially require the participation of women in community consultations. The EIA Decree can serve as a springboard for more gender responsive interventions, but without a suite of policy initiatives—as well as corresponding legislation to enforce commitments to gender equality—it remains to be seen how much it can positively impact women's resilience.

A notable characteristic of the Lao PDR legislation is that it routinely provides for formal equality between men and women, or the equal treatment of women and men. Many of the laws and policies reviewed for this report make no mention of men or women or gender. The underlying assumption is that if a law applies to everyone, then women and men should always be treated the same under that law. Consequently, many laws do not recognize or address the different roles, responsibilities, socioeconomic and cultural contexts, and backgrounds of women and girls or men and boys. To rectify this, the NAPGE needs to be leveraged and comprehensive sex-disaggregated data collected and analyzed to form the evidence base for decision making. This evidence base can be used to design laws and policies that address the differing experiences and challenges of women and men and ensure equality of outcomes, or substantive equality, in areas that affect resilience to climate change and disaster impacts.

CEDAW GR37 articulates a push for policy coherence and effective integration of gender equality within legislation and policies in sectors relevant to climate change and disaster risk. The framework developed for this report has provided an approach to identify laws and policies that impact the ability of women to build resilience to climate change and disasters. The gender scale adopted in the analysis is an important tool to understand across multiple sectors where gender has or has not yet been mainstreamed. Based on the results of this analysis, a series of recommendations have been made, both specific and general.

Specific Recommendations

Develop gender responsive guidance to accompany the Law on Gender Equality. The LGE currently lacks definitions of the essential concepts of equality (including both formal and substantive equality), or discrimination (both direct and indirect) as outlined in the CEDAW Convention. It is recommended that the government develop these definitions as guidance to accompany the LGE. This would lay the foundation for gender responsive measures in laws and policies which can be applied across sectors as gender mainstreaming progress under the NAPGE. The government could support this by integrating references to the LGE in all new laws and policies, including the National Strategy on Climate Change (2021–2030) and Five-Year National DRR Action Plan. It could also develop the grievance and complaint processes referenced in both the LGE and NAPGE and ensure that they are equipped to produce substantive gender equality. This guidance would support the gender responsive implementation of the LGE, complement the NAPGE, and strengthen links between the two by clarifying key implementation measures.

Support women's participation in decision making in the National Strategy on Climate Change (2021–2030), future reviews of the Climate Change (CC) Decree, and Environmental Protection Law. Women are significantly underrepresented in environmental decision making in the Lao PDR, and the CC Decree does not provide additional opportunities for women and other marginalized groups to participate in decision making or implementation relating to climate change. However, the NAPGE has set ambitious targets for women's participation and leadership in climate change decision making. In the forthcoming National Strategy on Climate Change (2021–2030)—and any future reviews of the CC Decree—the government could strengthen efforts to promote women's participation in climate change decision making through several measures: (i) mandate consultations with the NCAWMC, LWU and civil society organizations representing women as part of the creation of policies and guidelines on climate change; (ii) include measures such as capacity building for women policymakers and the establishment of quotas to support NAPGE Outputs 2.5 and 2.6 on women's participation in decision making and leadership roles on climate change; and (iii) require comprehensive gender mainstreaming in climate change mitigation and adaptation measures.

Integrate measures that support women's resilience into disaster risk reduction under the National Strategy on DRR (NSDRR) and the DM Law. An opportunity exists with the implementation of the DM Law and NSDRR—including the development of the 5-year national disaster risk reduction action plans—to elaborate on positive elements of the DM Law that provide for equality and address women's differential needs in the context of disasters. The NSDRR and the 5-year action plans provide opportunities to implement the DM Law in a gender responsive manner, by (i) ensuring women are present in the institutions as civil servants in decision-making roles, and as members of disaster management committees from central to village level; (ii) by conducting targeted capacity building for women civil servants and community leaders; and (iii) by collaborating with institutions to address women's differential needs in disaster contexts—such as the LWU, the NCAWMC, and the National Taskforce on the Prevention of Violence Against Women—to address the important issue of gender-based violence in disasters.

Support women's resilience through the right to live without violence with revisions to the Law on Preventing and Combatting Violence against Women and Children 2014 and strong implementation of the National Plan of Action on Protection and Elimination of Violence Against Women and Children (2021–2025). As of 2021, the law does not give clear guidance on an important question of women's access to justice when they experience family violence, and that is the use of alternative dispute resolution methods such as settlement, compromise, and mediation processes. The government could set rules in the law or develop regulations on how such mechanisms can be lawfully undertaken, along with a requirement for training and accreditation of any persons undertaking such processes. It will also be essential to ensure that the national plan of action includes capacity-building programs for judges, prosecutors, the police and other law enforcement officials, and members of village mediation units, to ensure that all cases of gender-based violence are investigated and prosecuted in a gender-sensitive manner as recommended by the CEDAW Committee 2018 in its concluding observations at paragraphs 24 and 26.

Enhance women's economic capacity through changes to the gender wage equality provisions in the Law on Labor 2014, by making a new law on prevention of harassment and violence in the workplace, and on investing in the development of women-led micro, small, and medium-sized enterprises (MSMEs). The gender pay gap means women have less access to economic resources for their work, and so less capacity to adapt to climate change or recover from disasters. A small revision to Article 96 of the Law on Labor could bring it up to the ILO Equal Remuneration Convention 100 standard by referring to "equal remuneration for work of equal value." Women's well-being and economic security are also impacted by harassment and violence in the workplace, and it is recommended that a special law be developed to define, prevent, and prohibit harassment and sexual harassment in employment and occupation in all its forms, with adequate sanctions and remedies. As many Lao women also work in MSMEs—both formal and informal—another important aspect of building their economic resilience is greater investment in resources, training, networking, and access to finance for women entrepreneurs, including for those combining business and career responsibilities, and women in rural areas.

Improve women's access to land, housing, assets, and agricultural resources through gender mainstreaming the Law on Land 2019, the Law on Resettlement and Vocation 2018, the Law on Forestry 2007, and the National Agro- Biodiversity Program and Action Plan (2021–2025). These main laws and policies on land, forest, resettlement, and agriculture do not take account of gender difference or promote equality in access to resources, and such change is needed in future revisions of these laws or in implementing decrees and sector strategies. Specifically, it is recommended that the Law on Land is amended to restore a right that existed in the previous version (Article 43 of the 2003 version), to register matrimonial land titles under the names of the husband and wife. On the National Agro-Biodiversity Program, it is recommended that detailed guidance is added on ways to incorporate gender into the implementation of the program and address the inequalities due to the gendered division of labor in agriculture and forestry. All of these legislative and policy changes in turn, will need to be underpinned by research on inheritance practices concerning women and girls inheriting property and housing, as well as the ownership and occupation of land, particularly for rural women.

General Recommendations

Collection and analysis of disaggregated data need to be prioritized. Noted as the first specific measure under CEDAW GR37, the collection and assessment of disaggregated data are critical to understanding the complex impacts of climate change and disaster risk. This report has demonstrated that as of 2021, there is little disaggregated data and evidence to identify gender-based vulnerabilities in the Lao PDR. Collection of data disaggregated by sex, age, disability, ethnicity, and geographical location at the minimum is recommended. The EIA Decree requirement for gender data and assessments provides a useful starting point for increasing provisions for the collection of gender and climate change and disaster related statistics in laws and policies, such as the NSDRR and the 5-year DRR action plans. The government could also benefit from the collection of more comprehensive national sex-disaggregated quantitative and qualitative data on land tenure and property ownership and inheritance practices, especially in rural areas. This would support the design of gender responsive measures to ensure women's equal rights to assets, especially in rural areas and the agriculture sector.

Increasing the participation of women in disaster risk reduction, action on climate change, and wider environmental decision making is essential. As of 2021, women have very little say over the policy formulation process due to the limited number of women in disaster and environmental decision-making positions at the central, provincial, district, and village levels, and a lack of mandates for gender-inclusive processes. The NAPGE stipulates specific provisions for increasing the participation and leadership of women in the development and implementation of national policies and plans on climate change and disaster risk reduction. Targeting sectors, such as agriculture, is key to strengthening the resilience of women to climate change and disasters. Efforts are also needed to increase the gender responsiveness of public participation in environmental policy. The EIA Decree provides a starting point as its stipulations for gender data and assessments essentially require the inclusion of women in community consultations. The government could build on the EIA Decree by making regulations on public participation and community consultations on environmental protection and approval of new projects, to require that consultation procedures and environmental management plans are gender responsive and provide clear guidance on how this is done. This can provide a standard for community and public participation that can be implemented at multiple levels to increase the voice of often marginalized groups such as women, those in rural areas, and people with disabilities.

Consolidate a gender responsive approach to climate change and disaster risk. It is recommended that the NEC and MoNRE, the National DM Committee, and MLSW collaborate with the NCAWMC to ensure that (i) all national policy processes, international compliance reports, and international climate finance proposals routinely include the achievement of gender equality as a key strategic objective; (ii) the institutions and processes include women staff and community leaders and women's organizations such as the LWU to support gender responsive capacity building for civil servants and community leaders in climate change and disaster risk reduction planning and implementation; and (iii) the policies include budget, gender indicators and monitoring in line with the SDGs as a whole, and especially SDG5 on gender equality and the empowerment of women and girls.

Glossary

Discrimination against girls and women: Any distinction, exclusion, or restriction made on the basis of sex which has the effect or purpose of impairing or nullifying the recognition, enjoyment, or exercise by women irrespective of their marital status, on the basis of equality of men and women, of human rights and fundamental freedoms in the political, economic, social, cultural civil or any other field. The definition includes not just **direct discrimination** (or intentional discrimination), but any act that has the effect of creating or perpetuating inequality between men and women which may be indirect discrimination.

Source: United Nations (UN) Women. 2017. *Gender Equality Glossary.*

Gender: Refers to the roles, behaviors, activities, and attributes that a given society at a given time considers appropriate for men and women. In addition to the social attributes and opportunities associated with being male and female and the relationships between women and men and girls and boys, gender also refers to the relations between women and those between men. These attributes, opportunities, and relationships are socially constructed and are learned through socialization processes. They are context time-specific and changeable. Gender determines what is expected, allowed, and valued in a woman or a man in a given context. In most societies, there are differences and inequalities between women and men in responsibilities assigned, activities undertaken, access to and control over resources, as well as decision making opportunities. Gender is part of the broader socio-cultural context, as are other important criteria for sociocultural analysis including class, race, poverty level, ethnic group, sexual orientation, age, etc. (see discrimination above).

Source: UN Women. 2017. *Gender Equality Glossary.*

Gender analysis: A critical examination of how differences in gender roles, activities, needs, opportunities and rights/entitlements affect men, women, girls, and boys in certain situations or contexts. Gender analysis examines the relationships between females and males and their access to and control of resources and the constraints they face relative to each other. A gender analysis should be integrated into all sector assessments or situational analyses to ensure that gender-based injustices and inequalities are not exacerbated by interventions and that where possible, greater equality and justice in gender relations are promoted.

Source: UN Women. 2017. *Gender Equality Glossary.*

Gender equality: Refers to the equal rights, responsibilities, and opportunities of women and men and girls and boys. Equality does not mean that women and men will become the same but that women's and men's rights, responsibilities, and opportunities will not depend on whether they are born male or female. Gender equality implies that the interests, needs, and priorities of both women and men are taken into consideration, recognizing the diversity of different groups of women and men. Gender equality is not a women's issue but should concern and fully engage men as well as women. Equality between women and men is seen both as a human rights issue and as a precondition for, and indicator of, sustainable people-centered development.

Source: UN Women. 2017. *Gender Equality Glossary.* Gender equality includes not only **formal equality** (de jure equality – treating men and women the same) but also includes **substantive equality** (de facto equality – equality of outcome in fact for both women and men).

Source: Convention on the Elimination of All Forms of Discrimination Against Women (CEDAW). 2004. *General Recommendations adopted by the Committee on the Elimination of Discrimination Against Women. General Recommendation No. 25.*

Gender mainstreaming: Gender mainstreaming is the chosen approach of the United Nations system and international community toward realizing progress on women's and girls' rights, as a subset of human rights to which the United Nations dedicates itself. It is not a goal or objective on its own. It is a strategy for implementing greater equality for women and girls in relation to men and boys. Mainstreaming a gender perspective is the process of assessing the implications for women and men of any planned action, including legislation, policies, or programs, in all areas and at all levels. It is a way to make women's as well as men's concerns and experiences an integral dimension of the design, implementation, monitoring, and evaluation of policies and programs in all political, economic, and societal spheres so that women and men benefit equally, and inequality is not perpetuated. The ultimate goal is to achieve gender equality.

Source: UN Women. 2017. *Gender Equality Glossary.*

Gender negative: Applies gender norms, roles, and stereotypes that reinforce gender inequalities.

Source: UN Women. 2017. *Gender Equality Glossary.*

Gender neutral: Gender is not considered relevant to outcomes.

Source: UN Women. 2017. *Gender Equality Glossary.*

Gender positive/transformative: Changes gender norms, roles and transforms unequal gender relations to promote shared power, control of resources, decision making, and support for women's empowerment.

Source: UN Women. 2017. *Gender Equality Glossary.*

Gender sensitive: Considers gender norms, roles, and relations taking into account sociocultural factors, but does not actively address gender inequalities.

Source: WHO. 2012. https://www.who.int/globalchange/publications/Mainstreaming_Gender_Climate.pdf.

Gender responsive: Pays attention to specific needs of women and men and intentionally uses gender considerations to affect the design, implementation, and results of legislation, policies, and programs.

Source: UNICEF. 2017. *Gender Equality Glossary of Terms and Concepts.*

9789292695798